POCKET
GARDENING
GUIDES

GARDEN
PROJECTS

❖

DAVID SQUIRE

POCKET
GARDENING
GUIDES

GARDEN PROJECTS

❖

DAVID SQUIRE

Illustrated by Vana Haggerty

TIGER BOOKS INTERNATIONAL
LONDON

Designed and conceived by

THE BRIDGEWATER BOOK COMPANY LTD

Art Directed by PETER BRIDGEWATER

Designed by TERRY JEAVONS

Illustrated by VANA HAGGERTY FLS

Edited by MARGOT RICHARDSON

CLB 3377

This edition published in 1994 by

TIGER BOOKS INTERNATIONAL PLC, London

© 1994 Colour Library Books Ltd,

Godalming, Surrey

Printed and bound in Singapore

ISBN 1-85501-379-7

CONTENTS

Garden leisure	*6–7*
Levelling and shaping the ground	*8–9*
Draining land	*10–11*
Making a concrete drive	*12–13*
Patio surfaces	*14–15*
Laying paving slabs	*16–17*
Laying pavers	*18–19*
Creating paths	*20–21*
Making steps	*22–23*
Brick walls	*24–25*
Screen-block walls	*26–27*
Dry-stone walls	*28–29*
Fences	*30–31*
Constructing a boarded fence	*32–33*
Gates	*34–35*
Trellises	*36–37*
Carports	*38–39*
Timber and brick pergolas	*40–41*
Rustic pergolas	*42–43*
Rock gardens	*44–45*
Making a pond with a liner	*46–47*
Making a pond with a pre-cast shell	*48–49*
Making a concrete pond	*50–51*
Making a waterfall	*52–53*
Making benches and tables	*54–55*
Making a barbeque	*56–57*
Compost bins and dustbins	*58–59*
Play areas	*60–61*
Useful garden project terms	*62–63*
Index	*64*

GARDEN LEISURE

 GARDENS should be fun, perhaps with an air of mystery and unpredictability, or even entertainment. There have, of course, been formal gardens – perhaps none more rigid and better known than Versailles with its clinical lines – but the country-garden theme has always been present, enabling medleys of flowers to jostle for position in borders.

PERSONAL TOUCHES
Every garden benefits from at least one amusing or eccentric feature to distinguish it from neighbouring territories. On a grand scale, follies and grottos are idiosyncratic, while in less expansive circumstances arbours, summerhouses and gazebos fulfil this function. Gnomes, miniature windmills and other garden ornaments also personalize areas within a garden – but to avoid an overpowering effect, select them with care. Stone animals, including cats, dogs and rabbits, are also popular and widely seen.

A pleasure garden depicted in the medieval poem 'Le Roman de la Rose' (The Romance of the Rose), an elaborate allegory on love and secular life. The garden is fenced with wattle.

Leisure and pleasure were pursued with vigour at Versailles, begun as a small hunting lodge by Louis XIII, and later expanded to create one of the largest, most lavish and best known of all gardens.

CONTEMPLATIVE CAVES

Grottos were initially places where the mysteries of the universe were contemplated; an extension of the caves in which the Greek philosopher Plato had reflected on life. Renaissance Italy first developed the use of grottos, followed by the French and the British in the eighteenth century.

Here are designs for grottos during the late 1700s. They became increasingly ornate, but were basically cave-like and full of mystery.

FOLLIES

These garden structures have, by definition, no purpose; even their name suggests a sense of foolishness and eccentricity. Early ones were Italian, but the English pursued the style with vigour and passion, creating whimsical and eccentric designs that required wealth and time to construct.

They are conspicuous by their lack of purpose and frequently took the form of sham ruins, arches and even mock churches. Towers were popular, as well as gazebos, pagodas and megaliths.

Many follies were built in the mid-eighteenth century and were usually complete structures. However, later ones, in the early nineteenth century, were whimsical treatments of park and farm buildings, including dairies, barns, ice-houses, kennels and bath-houses.

Many follies still exist, from stone circles and hermit cells, to bridges that go nowhere and mock churches. Perhaps their survival should not be too much of a surprise, as many were designed by architects. It is a continued bafflement to many people how the English could so seriously pursue futility and silliness.

GNOMES

Gnomes always captivate children, but their impression on adults is varied. Most modern gnomes are richly painted and bear a likeness to Walt Disney's dwarfs in Snow White, which themselves resemble woodcuts featured in a sixteenth century book on metallurgy. There are, however, local influences, and an antipodean variation sports a swaggie's hat.

In the nineteenth century, wrought-iron garden furniture encouraged the introduction of lighter and more ornate designs than earlier, cast-iron styles allowed.

LEVELLING AND SHAPING THE GROUND

CREATING the desired levels in a new plot of land is fundamental to its design, and unless these are right you will never be completely satisfied with the garden. It does, however, often involve moving soil from one area to another, which is heavy, labour-intensive work. Therefore, once an area immediately around a house is levelled or terraced, allow the rest of the garden to assume its natural contour.

TO ENSURE *an area is level in all directions, knock in 23cm/9in-long pegs about 1.5m/5ft apart. First, however, mark each peg, 10cm/4in from its top. Use a spirit-level to ensure they are at the same height, then rake the soil level with the marks.*

PRECIOUS TOPSOIL

There is always the risk, when levelling soil, of mixing topsoil with the subsoil, or totally inverting them so that the surface is covered with sticky clay. Therefore, first remove the surface soil. This may appear tedious, but annuals, herbaceous perennials and alpine plants especially will not thrive in thick clay. Many shrubs and trees are more tolerant of such conditions, but even they will not perform well there. If the area is totally formed of clay, buy in clean, fresh topsoil.

ASSESSING LEVELS

This needs 23cm/9in-long, flat-topped pegs, a builder's spirit-level, a straight, uniformly-thick plank about 1.8m/6ft long to rest it on, and a club hammer for knocking in the pegs. Levelling nearly flat areas is relatively easy, and is shown above.

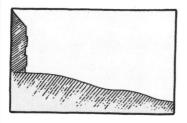

IF GROUND *slopes around a house, it is usually more convenient to form several terraces than to leave a steep bank. It is essential that the level of the top terrace is below the damp course on the house.*

THE ART *in making a terrace is not to move more soil than is necessary. Immediately around a house this may not be possible, as it is desirable to have only one or two steps' difference between each level.*

SUBSEQUENT *levels, however, are formed by taking soil from the upper half to fill the lower part. Remove the topsoil, so that good soil is not buried. This is vital where plants are to be grown.*

CREATE *a uniform slope by knocking pegs into the ground, 1.5m/5ft apart. Place a spirit-level across the top two pegs; knock in the lower peg until the required slope is formed. Mark the bubble's position on the spirit-level. Repeat this down the slope, each time leaving the bubble in the same place.*

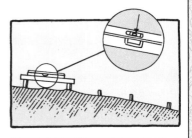

AN ALTERNATIVE *way to produce an even slope is to place a piece of wood under the lower end of the spirit-level to represent the amount of slope between any two pegs. When using the spirit-level, the bubble must be in the centre. Repeat this process with the next two pegs.*

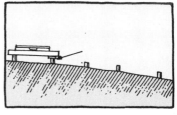

A FURTHER *way to create an even slope is to knock pegs into the soil at equal distances apart. Use a spirit-level to ensure they are all at the same height. Then, mark progressively increasing distances from their tops. The soil can then be sloped by making the surface touch these marks.*

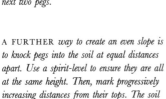

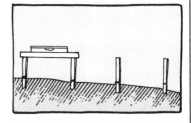

CONTOURING LAND

An alternative to levelling large areas is to form dells or slightly sloping banks. Unless grassed, avoid creating banks with angles of more than 30 degrees, as the soil may be too easily eroded. If grassed, consider how the bank will be cut – hover-type mowers are ideal for this.

When forming sunken gardens, always ensure the drainage is adequate, especially if a pond is planned in its base. Should it overflow through rain or water draining into it, the fish will be washed out. In such areas, it is better to consider a 'bog' garden, perhaps planted with moisture-loving primulas.

Take advantage of natural hollows and mounds within a garden, as these introduce character, and the opportunity to create features not possible in totally flat areas.

USING HOSE-PIPES

Assessing differences in levels over long distances is difficult without specialized equipment. However, home gardeners can use hose-pipes. Secure the top of each end to a peg at the upper level, then fill with water until both ends of the pipe are full. Measure the height of the water to give the difference in level. Putting a piece of plastic tubing in each end makes it easier to see the levels.

DRAINING LAND

$\diamond$

IDEALLY, soil should be free-draining, yet retain moisture. If it is totally saturated with water, this prevents air penetration and stops roots and soil organisms breathing. If this happens, drains need to be installed.

ASSESSING GARDENS

Large puddles of water remaining on the surface clearly indicate the need for drains. So, too, do the presence of rushes and sedges. If these are not readily apparent, but you wish to check the level of water in the soil (water-table), dig a 1.2m/4ft deep hole in autumn and see how much water remains in it during winter. If water stays in it and within 23cm/9in of the top for long periods, the installation of drains is essential.

RANGE OF DRAINS

There are several ways to drain land. On a large scale, it is possible to install 'mole' drains by mechanically (usually using a special tractor) drawing a metal, bullet-headed spike through the

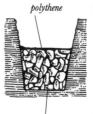

polythene

clean, coarse rubble

RUBBLE *drains are cheaper than tile types. Prepare trenches in the same way and fill to within 30cm/12in of the surface with rubble. Then, cover with double-thickness polythene.*

ground, 45–75cm/1½–2½ft below the surface. In suburban gardens this is not practical, and drainage relies on clay pipes, rubble drains or a continuous plastic type of drain.

• <u>Pipe drains</u> involve digging a main trench that leads to a sump or ditch. At intervals, side drains join it and gather water from a larger area. The spacings between the side drains depend on the soil's nature: 3.6–4.5m/12–15ft for clay soil, to 12m/40ft on light sandy types. Dig the trenches 60–75cm/2–2½ft deep and 30–45cm/1–1½ft wide, with a minimum slope of 1 in 90 towards

INSTALL *pipe drains by digging trenches with a slight slope. Form a 7.5–10cm/ 3–4in-thick layer of gravel and place the pipes on top. Link in the side drains and cover joints with double-thickness polythene.*

COVER *the joints and pipes with gravel. Alternatively, cover them with broken pieces of tile. Then, spread gravel over the pipes and tiles. This prevents soil seeping into the pipes and eventually blocking them.*

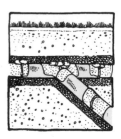

THE *life expectancy of pipe drains depends on the thoroughness with which they are installed. Fill the trench with topsoil and firm it level with the surface. It may settle, so be prepared to add further soil later.*

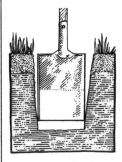

DIG *out a trench to the depth and width of a spade when laying the relatively new, rectangular, plastic-type drains. They are formed of a continuous plastic core which is surrounded by a porous fibre.*

ON MODERATELY *heavy soil the plastic can be laid directly on the trench's base and covered with soil. On heavy land, however, mix sharp sand or gravel with soil immediately around the tube to aid water flow.*

FILL THE *trench with soil and firm it with a foot. Leave the soil slightly proud of the surface to allow for slight soil settlement. Direct the end of the pipe into a ditch or sump, where water can drain freely.*

the outlet. Place a spirit-level on top of the pipes to check that they slope in the right direction. Laying pipe drains is illustrated on the opposite page.

Main drains are formed of unglazed clay pipes, about 30cm/12in long and 13cm/5in wide, while the side, feeder ones are the same length but only 10cm/4in wide.

• Rubble drains are cheaper than pipe types, and ideal where builders have left a great deal of broken bricks and other clean rubble on the site. Prepare the trenches in exactly the same way as for pipe drains. Their life expectancy is less than with pipe drains, as eventually soil seeps among the rubble and clogs up spaces through which water could drain. However, even pipe drains have a limited life if trees such as willows are nearby: their roots soon can cause blockages.

For both pipe and rubble drains, the widths of the trench may vary: machines can dig deeper and narrower than a man using a spade and shovel.

• Plastic drains are formed of a continuous core surrounded by porous fabric. It is bought in lengths several metres long and easily laid in the base of a narrow trench. Only on heavy, clay soils does it need to be laid with gravel surrounding it. The technique of installing it is described at the top of this page.

SUMP OR DITCH?

Some gardens have ditches into which excess water can drain, but most do not. It is illegal to drain surplus soil water into domestic drainage systems, and therefore a sump is needed. At the lowest point, dig a hole about 1.2m/4ft square, making its base about 30cm/12in below the pipe that takes water into it. Fill the sump to about half its depth with clean, coarse rubble, then with gravel to about 30cm/12in below the surface. Cover with double-thickness polythene, then with topsoil and, finally, turf.

MAKING A CONCRETE DRIVE
❖

CONCRETE is an adaptable material, flexible before it is set, and so able to be formed into a wide range of shapes. When dry, it creates a strong, hard-wearing surface. Its strength is derived as much from the thorough preparation of the foundations as from its thickness and ratio of Portland cement to sharp sand and aggregates.

PREPARING THE SITE
Careful preparation of the site is essential.
• Remove all plants and rubbish.
• Dig out the topsoil, placing it in an out-of-the-way position.
• Concrete can be laid directly on most well-compacted ground, but if the soil is mainly formed of clay a 10cm/4in-thick layer of compacted, broken bricks or stones is needed. Ensure this layer is free from rubbish: spread 15cm/6in wider than the area to be concreted.

ROMAN INFLUENCE

Mortar was created as early as two thousand years ago by the Romans. But instead of using Portland cement – first introduced in the nineteenth century – they employed lime.

• Construct a framework of strong, straight-topped wood around the area, so that a space is left to create a slab of concrete 6–7.5cm/2¹/₂–3in thick. Support the framework with strong pegs knocked into the ground on the outside. Their tops must be below the framework, and securely nailed to it.
• If the drive is long, it is necessary to split it up to prevent cracking later when it expands as a result of high temperatures. As a guide, no area should be longer than 3m/10ft. The wood used to separate the area should join the outer framework at right-angles.

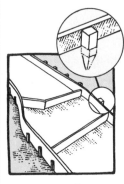

1. CONCRETE *forms a strong base, but it can look bland and unexciting unless given an attractive finish. First, form a strong framework around the sides, with pegs holding it secure. Divide large areas into several parts to allow for expansion.*

2. BUYING *ready-mixed concrete in bulk is an easy and quick way to create a base. However, ensure there is a team of at least five people to help: three to barrow the concrete and two to level and lay it. Buy 10% more than you need.*

3. HAND-MIXING *is the cheapest way to mix concrete, but can be heavy work if the area is large. To create a strong surface it must be laid continuously, so ensure that one mix of concrete does not become dry before the next one is added.*

SURFACE TEXTURES

These are made before the concrete has set, using wooden floats, trowels and shovels.

1. *Using a soft brush*
2. *Soft brush plus water*
3. *The back of a shovel*
4. *Wooden float*
5. *Steel trowel*

1 *Soft lines*

2 *Gritty surface*

3 *Rustic and circled*

4 *Sandpaper texture*

5 *Smooth and flat*

LAYING CONCRETE

Never lay concrete if the weather is frosty, extremely hot or if it is likely to rain before setting.

• If the base area is dry, water it before laying the concrete.

• First, place concrete around dividing strips of wood.

• Start laying concrete at the end furthest from the mixer or supply, and follow the information below.

• Use a mixture (by volume) of:

~1 part Portland cement
~1¹/₂ parts sharp sand
~2¹/₂ parts 20mm aggregate
(Alternatively, use a mixture
of 3¹/₂ parts combined aggregate
to one of Portland cement)

4. ELECTRICALLY-OPERATED *mixers can be hired: choose one with a capacity of about 100 litres. Machine mixing removes much of the hard work but does need a team of at least three people if the cost of hiring is to be economic.*

5. SPREAD *the concrete, packing it well around the edges, then level but leave it slightly higher than the wooden surround. Use a tamping beam to compact and level the surface. This is a two-man job and involves pushing and pulling.*

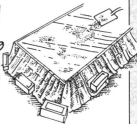

6. WHEN *the concrete has hardened slightly, cover it with polythene sheeting to prevent rapid drying. Secure the sheeting at the sides with bricks, as well as lightly sprinkling sand on the surface to prevent it 'ballooning'.*

PATIO SURFACES

❖

IN RECENT years, the range of materials available for forming patios, terraces and the surrounds to houses has become much wider and decorative.

The Romans constructed ornate, mosaic pathways, while in the late 1800s wood blocks cut from the Australian Jarrah Tree (*Eucalyptus marginata*) were used in London to form roads and other surfaces. In the early and mid-1900s, the choice of surfacing materials included natural paving, plainly coloured pre-cast slabs, or bricks or rafts of concrete; but in recent years the range has widened dramatically and now there are surfacing materials in textures, shapes and sizes to suit everyone's taste.

PAVING SLABS

Pre-cast paving slabs are man-made and have a uniform outline: square, rectangular, hexagonal or round. They can be laid on their own or in combination with bricks or cobbles. Indeed, although paving slabs may not initially appear to be an inspiring choice, when used in combination with other materials and attractive edgings they can be given plenty of eye-appeal.

Slabs with raised, patterned surfaces create added interest and can, if spaces are left between them for plants, be given an informal appearance at a fraction of the cost of using natural stone.

NATURAL STONE

Stone is expensive to buy and, because of its uneven thickness, difficult to lay. Nevertheless, when laid it has an attractive quality that is unsurpassed in natural and informal settings.

Part of the beauty of this material is its characteristic non-uniform outlines and surfaces, but some slabs, such as sawn sandstone, are available in a clinically-cut form; while for a slightly less rigid outline they are sold 'dressed'. When the stone has an irregular outline it is called 'random'.

COTTAGE *gardens need informal patios, preferably formed from natural, irregularly-shaped stone paving. Gaps can be left between them in which small, prostrate plants can be set, such as thyme.*

MODERN *houses harmonize with square or rectangular paving slabs, in a range of bright colours. Choose symmetrically-shaped, plastic, glass-fibre or concrete containers to complete the somewhat formal scene.*

WEATHERED, *square or rectangular flag-stones create semi-informal patios. Lay them irregularly, so that there is no clear pattern. Wooden troughs and ornate pots harmonize in this informal and rustic setting.*

PAVERS

House-type bricks have been used to create paths in cottage gardens for several centuries, but in regions where winters are wet and extremely cold they soon disintegrate. Nowadays, weather-resistant bricks are available. (Some are interlocking; others just butted together.) They do not have to be laid on a concrete base or with mortar; instead, they are bedded on an evenly compacted layer of sharp sand. This creates an attractive, stable surface, but it is essential that the area is surrounded by a brick or wood framework that restrains the bed of sand. Indeed, if strong edgings are omitted, the sand will spread at the edges and the pavers collapse.

GRANITE SETTS

These are grey quarried stone, extremely hard, either brick-shaped or square, and about the size of a half-brick. Take care not to use too many of them as they have a dominant appearance. Rather, employ them as a decorative contrast with other materials. They are laid on a mortar base.

PAVING MATERIALS
Paving slabs and bricks, with formal or informal outlines, are widely used to create attractive surfaces. Most patios are totally formed of one type, while others are attractive combinations of two or three.

CONCRETE *slabs with raised patterns. Several attractive colours.*

HEXAGONAL *and round slabs with smooth surfaces. Several colours.*

SQUARE, *brick-coloured slabs marked in brick-like and square patterns.*

IRREGULARLY *shaped, natural stone slabs create informal patios.*

GRANITE *setts create hard-wearing surfaces for informal areas.*

COBBLES *are eye-catching but are best combined with other surfaces.*

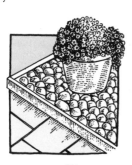

LARGE *cobble-stones create ornamental areas that are difficult to walk on, but ideal as positions for plants in tubs. It safeguards them from passers-by knocking and damaging the flowers or foliage.*

INTERLOCKING *pavers create a strong, hard-wearing surface.*

BRICK *pavers are hard-wearing and laid on bed of evenly compacted sand.*

LAYING PAVING SLABS

❖

Store slabs by standing them on wooden slats and leaning against a firm surface.

PRE-CAST paving slabs create firm patio surfaces, either on their own or when combined with materials such as bricks. They range in thickness from 42–50mm/ 1³/4–2in; and the most common size is 45cm/1¹/2ft square – as well as quarter and half sizes so that patterns can be formed. Plain slabs 60cm/2ft square and 75cm/2¹/2ft by 60cm/2ft are available, but are difficult to handle.

DAMP COURSES

Where patios adjoin buildings, they must be at least 15cm/6in below the damp course. If this is impossible, leave a 10cm/4in gap between the slabs and the wall, to a depth of 15cm/6in below the damp course. Fill this area with 6mm/¹/4in pea-shingle. If this is omitted, there is a risk of damp passing into the building.

CREATING A FIRM BASE

Where paving slabs are being laid as a path that will not have people continuously walking – and, with children, jumping – on it, laying them on a bed of mortar is not essential. Just lay them on a 5cm/2in-thick layer of sharp sand. However, if the area is around a house and expected to be in use throughout the year, form a sharp-sand base and bed the slabs on a mixture of:

~

1 part Portland cement
3 parts soft sand

~

The technique of laying them is described below.

Where slabs are to be laid on clay soil, first form a 10cm/4in-thick, well-compacted hardcore base. Over this, form a 5cm/2in-thick layer of evenly consolidated sharp sand, then lay the slabs on the above mortar mix. If the area is large and will be in continual use, form a 6–7.5cm/2–2¹/2in-thick concrete base over the hard-core, using a mixture of:

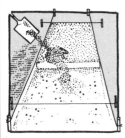

REMOVE *plants and rubbish from the site. To ensure the patio's surface will be right, it may be necessary to excavate some soil. Mark out the area and spread a 5cm/2in-thick layer of sharp sand.*

FIRM *the sand and rake level. First, lay slabs along the longest, highest side (there should be a gentle slope). One way to lay a slab is to form a 36–50mm/1¹/2– 2in ridge of mortar in a box-like formation.*

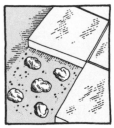

ALTERNATIVELY, *use the five-blob method, setting one 36–50mm/1¹/2–2in high mound in the centre and four others, at each corner. This is a quicker method than the box formation and uses less mortar.*

1 part Portland cement
2¹/2 parts sharp sand
3¹/2 parts 20mm aggregate

~

Lay the slabs on top using the 'blob' or 'box' method.

MIXING AND MATCHING

Patios should be as visually exciting as the rest of the garden. Indeed, as they are permanent features, careful planning and a great deal of thought is needed to ensure they both harmonize with the house, and have distinctive features. Here are a few simple ways to create a unique patio:

• If the area is large, leave out a few slabs at random and fill the area with cobbles or gravel. Use these gaps to direct people to steps and other features, rather than blocking their paths.

• Between every large paving slab (or four smaller ones) build in weather-resistant bricks, either revealing their backs or sides. Continue this brick theme into a surrounding wall.

• Omit a slab and cement a central pillar of a circular table into its middle. Then, fill the remaining part of the area with cobbles.

CUTTING SLABS

To cut a slab, first score across both faces. Then, using a bolster chisel and club-hammer, progressively chip away at the surface. Alternatively, use a powered tool called a disc-cutter. Wear gloves and goggles while using it.

• Leave out four or six slabs and construct a raised garden pond. This could be in the centre of the patio, or merged at one side of the area into a small wall.

• Omit two or three slabs and form a raised flower bed. This is ideal for people in wheelchairs.

• Position a statue towards one side of the patio and introduce lights to create a focal point.

GENTLY *set the slab in position. Slabs 45cm/1¹/2ft square are easily lifted by one person, but ones 60cm/ 2ft square – or larger – require two pairs of hands if they are to be set down evenly on the mortar.*

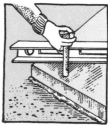

USE A *builder's spirit-level to ensure there is a slight slope in one direction. If slight adjustment is needed, tap with the handle of a club-hammer. If a radical change is needed, it is easier to remove the slab.*

AFTER *the mortar holding the slabs is set, fill the gaps with a stiff, dry, weak, mortar mixture, well rammed into the joints until fractionally below the slabs. Use a damp sponge to clean the edges of the slabs.*

LAYING PAVERS

◆

THESE are relatively new and increasingly popular. They are also known as concrete paving blocks and are widely used for paths, drives and patio areas. There are several different patterns in which they can be laid, illustrated below. Where they are being used for drives and hard-wearing surfaces, the herringbone pattern is best, but for small areas on terraces and patios the parquet design (sometimes known as basket weave) is less baffling to the eye. If a running-bond pattern (see below) is used for drives, it must run across the main line of traffic.

PREPARING THE SITE

Laying pavers does not involve the use of Portland cement or mortar: instead, the blocks are laid on a bed of sharp sand. It is therefore essential that the sand is restrained to prevent it escaping and the surface collapsing, especially at its edges. Sometimes there is a wall that can be used on one side, but usually either wooden, brick or concrete edges have to be constructed to restrain the sand.

Ensure vegetation and rubbish is removed, as well as the topsoil. If the area is to be a drive, a 10cm/4in-thick base formed of evenly consolidated hardcore is essential to help spread and support the load. Clay soils need the same treatment. When laying pavers it is essential to hire a mechanical plate vibrator to settle them into position: this can also be used to consolidate hardcore.

The pavers are about the size of house bricks and available in several thicknesses: 60mm/2$\frac{1}{2}$in or 65mm/2$\frac{3}{4}$in is suitable for patios and lightly trafficked areas, whereas ones 80mm/3$\frac{1}{2}$in thick are essential where lorries pass over the surface.

Construct the restrainer around the site so that it is 10cm/4in above the hardcore. Sharp sand is then spread and levelled (without consolidating it) by using a scraping

PAVERS *can be laid in many attractive patterns that help to give surfaces added interest. This is a herring-bone pattern and is especially suitable for hard-wearing, informal and irregularly-shaped areas.*

THE *running-bond pattern is fairly easy to lay but is not really suitable for hard-wearing areas. If used for paths or drives, lay the pavers across the area and not lengthwise. Always stagger the joints.*

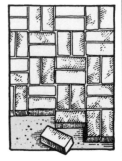

THE *parquet pattern is easy to lay if the area is square or rectangular and kept in multiples of 20cm/8in (the length of a brick). However, it is not a strong bond and may shift if used on a drive. It is ideal as a path.*

1. REMOVE *plants, rubbish and topsoil. If the area is clay or for cars, form and consolidate a 10cm/4in hardcore base between side restraining boards.*

2. SPREAD *sharp sand over the first metre/yard of the site. Strike this 45mm below the edge if using 60mm thick blocks, 50mm if laying 65mm pavers.*

3. DO NOT *stand on the sand, then start laying the pavers from the end nearest the supply. Stand on a wooden plank to prevent unnecessary disturbance.*

4. DEPENDING *on the pattern in which the pavers are laid, cutting is necessary. The easiest way is to hire a stone-splitter.*

5. USE *a plate vibrator (available from tool-hire shops) to bed the pavers into the sand. Two or three passes are needed – keep the vibrator moving.*

6. BRUSH *a thin layer of sharp sand over the pavers, making two or three further passes with the vibrator. Later, brush the surface, and lightly water.*

board (see illustration two). If 60mm/2½in-thick pavers are used, leave the sand's surface 45mm/1¾in below the restraining board's top. When using 65mm/2¾in-thick pavers, leave it 50mm/2in below the edges. These measurements allow for later consolidation of the pavers. Do not lay the sand more than a metre/yard or so in front of paver-laying area.

LAYING PAVERS

Start at the end where the pavers are stacked. Decide on the pattern to be used and begin at one corner. Position the bricks one at a time, just gently resting them on the sharp sand. Use a plank to spread your weight and systematically work down the area. When about 2.4m/8ft has been laid, use the vibrator to compact them, passing over the surface two or three times. Keep the machine moving except when switched off.

Use an hydraulic stone-splitter to cut the bricks – essential with the herringbone pattern.

When the area is complete and the bricks bedded into the sand by the vibrator, spread a thin layer of sharp sand over the surface and make two or three passes of the vibrator. Finish off by spreading sharp sand with a broom and then lightly watering the surface through a fine-rosed watering-can. The surface can then be used.

CREATING PATHS

FIRM, all-weather surfaces are essential in gardens, enabling access to sheds, greenhouses, fuel stores and garages throughout the year and in all weathers. Also, there needs to be a good path around a house to enable regular maintenance.

At one time, domestic pressure ensured that new gardens were instantly designed: washing lines were immediately needed and therefore two poles were installed with a line and path between them, away from walls, fences and overhanging trees. The path and washing line then dominated the garden for generations. Nowadays, clothes driers have changed all of this and garden design is much more flexible. New trends and materials have also encouraged the introduction of more attractive and interestingly shaped paths.

INNOVATIVE PATHS

Concrete gives superb all-weather paths but there are other choices,

many medleys of several materials. Here are a few to consider:

• <u>Stepping stones</u> in lawns have traditionally been formed from irregularly shaped, broken paving slabs. But slices of tree trunks also make paths: not through lawns but across areas covered with pea-shingle and with pots and tubs displayed on them.

• <u>Ordinary concrete paving slabs</u>, about 60cm/2ft square, can be made into an attractive path by spacing them 10cm/4in apart, forming wooden or concrete sides 30cm/12in on either side and filling the areas between them with gravel or small pebbles.

• <u>Gravel paths</u> with logs along their edges are especially attractive in informal settings. The path, however, has to be relatively flat to prevent the gravel gradually moving downhill.

• <u>Grass paths</u> are attractive, either straight and totally formed of grass, or combined with a log edging and used in informal settings. Strimmers have made edging grass close to logs very easy and have

1. REMOVE *plants, rubbish and topsoil. Mark the area with strings and add an even layer of clean rubble or stones. Compact it with a roller. Alternatively, ram it with the end of a heavy, vertical plank.*

2. USE *strong, 2.5cm/1in-thick timber to construct frameworks on either side of the path. Use a spirit-level to check they are level and allow for a 6–7.5cm/ 2¹/₂–3in-thick layer of concrete to be created.*

3. MIXING *concrete by hand is best if the path is short; if long, hire a cement-mixer. Spread cement, working it against the sides of the framework and initially leaving it about 2.5cm/1in higher.*

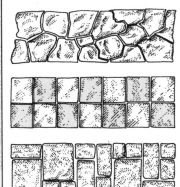

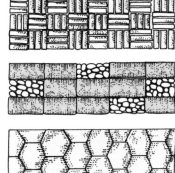

removed the earlier impracticalities of this design.

• <u>Unedged gravel paths</u> have a soft, unassuming texture that harmonizes with plants that spill over their edges. Constructing them is not difficult: dig out and remove the surface soil to about 7.5cm/3in deep. Then, fork over the top, 15cm/6in deep, and generously add cement powder. Mix it with the surface soil. Walk over the area, ram down the soil and then water it generously. Finally, cover with 5cm/2in of gravel.

• <u>Narrow, crazy-paving paths</u> are often bewildering to the eye, but if made slightly wider and with

CONCRETE forms functional paths, ideal in vegetable gardens but not sufficiently attractive for most ornamental areas. Existing paths that are in good condition can be improved by creating attractive surfaces on top of them.

---

bays for plants in tubs and other containers staggered along their sides, they assume a better dimension. Crazy paving is an adaptable material and can be used to fill oddly shaped corners in a way square or rectangular paving slabs do not allow. But they need a firm base to create a strong surface.

4. USE *a straight-edged board to level the surface. Draw it along the frameworks, at the same time tamping to ensure the concrete is compacted. Occasionally, draw the wood forward to remove excess.*

5. FOR *paths, use a mixture of 1 part Portland cement, $1^1/2$ parts sharp sand, and $2^1/2$ parts aggregate. Do not lay concrete during frosty weather (it might freeze) or when very hot (it dries too quickly).*

6. IMPROVE *the surface's appearance by using a stiff broom. Wait until it is nearly set, then brush vigorously to create a rough-textured surface. There are also some other surfaces (see page 13).*

MAKING STEPS

❖

WELL-PROPORTIONED steps can be a major feature in a garden, acting as a link between two levels and having a unifying influence. They must, at the same time, harmonize with the nature of the garden.

The proportions of steps is important and in general the riser (vertical distance) should be 15cm/6in high and the tread about 38cm/15in, with an overhang at the front of the step of about 5–7.5cm/2–3in.

Most steps are constructed from pre-fabricated slabs and bricks, but unique ones can be created from a wide range of materials:
• Log steps are popular in rustic and informal gardens, especially in naturalized and wild areas. Use logs 10–15cm/4–6in thick and cut to the width of the path. Excavate a shallow trench so that the log is buried about 5cm/2in to stabilize it. Additionally, use stout pegs to secure them into position. As well as the logs providing a rise in height, the path between them can rise or fall.

> ### SLOPES
>
> *As well as steps, slopes are important if someone in your family is wheelchair bound or needs to use a walking stick. Consider a gently curved slope that unites all levels. Avoid forming slopes greater than one in twelve.*

• Cross-sections of tree trunks – about 45cm/18in across and 10–15cm/4–6in thick – look superb when slightly overlapped and used to form a flight of steps. Pack soil around them to secure their positions. Take care when using them in wet weather, as they can be slippery.
• Railway sleepers create excellent steps. Cut them to the required width, bury slightly and use pegs to secure them and prevent movement. Avoid making the complete treads of wood, as they will then be very slippery, especially if covered with moss.

1. PAVING *slabs and bricks enable steps to be quickly constructed. At the base of the slope, lay a couple of slabs on compacted sand and mortar. Then, cement in place one layer of bricks to form the riser.*

2. USE *a spade to excavate the next step, forming a layer of sand and cementing the next slab in place. This is called the tread and should be about 38cm/15in long. Ensure each slab is firm and level.*

3. FORM *the next row of bricks that create the riser and repeat the laying of another slab to produce the tread. Continue like this until the flight of steps is complete. Place a further row of slabs at the top.*

1. SOMETIMES, *retaining walls that separate one level from another are too long and steps are needed. First, mark out the area with strings, excavate the soil and use bricks to build the first riser.*

2. MEASURE *from the front, and build the second riser 38cm/15in from the front. By using 45cm/18in-wide slabs, this allows for a 38cm/18in tread and an overlap at the front of about 7.5cm/3in.*

3. COMPLETE *the top riser and then put the slabs in place. Use a mixture of 1 part Portland cement and 3 of soft sand. It may be necessary to cut or replace the ornamental stones along the top of the wall.*

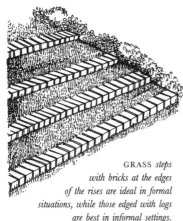

GRASS *steps with bricks at the edges of the rises are ideal in formal situations, while those edged with logs are best in informal settings.*

• Grass terraces and steps were widely used on a grand scale in the late 1800s to create dramatic effects. On a smaller scale, however, they also attract attention. Bricks or logs are used to form the risers and to prevent erosion during wet seasons. In formal situations, regular grass cutting is essential to create a uniform outline. In informal situations, however, where logs are used as the risers to steps, the grass can be left slightly longer. Strimmers help to keep the steps tidy.

• Clinical steps – where treads do not overhang the risers – harmonize well with modern architecture. Such steps can be made by setting a series of bricks on their sides and forming them into flights.

• Large rock gardens – or even a series of narrow, waterfall cascades – can be more effective with a series of random steps alongside them. Use the same type of stone as used in the rock garden, perhaps with areas of shingle between them.

• Old, spiral, metal staircases are decorative and can be used in basement gardens and are superb when covered with ivy – even if they do not go anywhere!

LOG *steps are ideal in informal, naturalized gardens. Secure the rises with stout pegs.*

BRICK WALLS

◆

Bricks are the units from which most houses are constructed, and they are also excellent for building garden walls. They are adaptable and can be formed into walls one or two bricks thick and up to about 1.8m/6ft high.

The life expectancy of a brick wall depends on several factors: the depth of the footings; quality of bricks; thickness and type of bond used; care taken during construction; and the installation of a water-proof capping at its top.

FOUNDATIONS

The depth of the foundations depends on the type of soil and the load they are to carry. Walls built on soils such as clay with a high water content clearly need deeper foundations than those on well-drained, gravelly soils. In most cases, however, trenches excavated 45–60cm/1½–2ft deep, initially filled with 10cm/4in of compacted hardcore, and then with a mixture of 1 part Portland cement, 2½ parts sharp sand and 3½ parts of 20mm aggregate to at least 15cm/6in thick, are suitable. The foundation's width must be at least three times the wall's thickness. Damp courses are essential to prevent ground moisture rising through the bricks.

RANGE OF BRICKS

There are three types of brick suitable for use in walls:
• Common bricks are general-purpose building types and used where appearance is not vital. They have no special facing side and are best when rendered or painted. Do not use them to support heavy loads or where they are subjected to stress. They are the cheapest type of brick.
• Facing bricks produce an attractive finish and are made in several colours and finishes, including rough and smooth. Mostly, these are either hand finished or have wire-cut, weather-resistant finishes on the sides and ends only.
• Engineering bricks are dense, smooth and impervious to water, making them ideal for use where a wall is partly buried or exposed to damp conditions.

LAYING *bricks is an age-old craft. It is based on the fact that mortar – a mixture of soft sand and cement or lime, or a combination – bonds one brick to another. Use a mixture of 1 part cement to 3 of soft sand.*

A LONG, *builder's spirit-level is essential to ensure courses of bricks are level and the structure upright. Keep the level clean, do not drop it and regularly check newly-laid bricks while the mortar is soft.*

LAY *bricks at both ends of the course, then tightly stretch a line between them to ensure the wall is not constructed with a bulge. Lay bricks so that they are staggered and vertical joints not continued from one course to another.*

RANGE OF BONDS

These are varied and complex and can create exceptionally attractive walls. For novice brick layers, however, the choice is between the 'running bond' when building a wall one-brick thick, or 'English bond' for a double one. With the 'running bond', after laying one course the next one starts half-a-brick in from the end, so that the vertical joints are staggered. For the 'English bond', every other row is laid across the wall, the other one along it, two bricks side by side. In all cases, lay bricks with the frog (side with the depression) downwards.

WALLS need not be plain and unappealing. Creating patterns with differently coloured and textured bricks introduces eye-appeal.

NATURAL stones create walls that often harmonize with local buildings. Use large blocks at the corners to create rigidity.

CONSTRUCTIONAL CARE

Ensuring the courses of bricks are level and upright encourages long life. Once the wall starts to lean, collapse soon follows. To ensure water does not penetrate through the mortar, point the joints. This involves waiting until the mortar has slightly stiffened, then using a small trowel to create a slope so that its lower side is level with the top of the lower brick but the upper side is partly recessed. Alternatively, run the end of a plastic hosepipe along the mortar.

DOUBLE-BRICK walls are strong and long-lasting. Make them even more attractive by covering with unusual cappings.

CAPPING

To prevent rainwater seeping down into the wall, either use facing bricks, shaped concrete slabs or attractively shaped tiles. These often help to create an attractive, distinctive wall.

AS WELL *as using a builder's spirit-level to ensure courses are level and upright, use it at an angle across the face of the wall to check for bulges. A long, straight-edged board can also be used for this purpose.*

HALF-BRICKS *are needed to fill gaps. First, lightly score around them with a bolster chisel. Place the brick on a bed of sand before using the chisel and club-hammer: angle the chisel towards the waste part.*

USE *a gauge rod (made from a piece of straight wood marked in brick-plus-mortar increments) to check that courses are rising consistently along its full length. Regularly check levels and vertical lines.*

SCREEN-BLOCK WALLS

❖

ARGE, pre-cast concrete, open-screen walling blocks are excellent for creating ornamental walls without totally blocking off light. They are 30cm/12in square and 10cm/4in thick, with either square or rounded designs within them. Some of these contain a single design, while other designs are revealed when four or more blocks are put together. Blocks cannot be cut, and there are neither half nor quarter sizes.

DESIGN FACTORS

Because these blocks are stack bonded (one immediately on top of another) walls constructed from them do not have great strength. Strong piers are needed at either end, and walls over 3m/10ft long need additional supports. As well as creating walls solely formed of them, they can also be set into solid brick walls, perhaps at eye-height to enable views to distant parts of a garden.

Unlike solid walls and fences, screen-block walling allows a flow of air which during summer can be especially welcome. However, avoid creating vast walls from them as they can look rather boring on their own. Climbers, as well as wall shrubs, can eliminate this problem.

The clinical nature of this walling enables it to blend well with patios formed of pre-cast square or rectangular paving, as well as cobbles. Indeed, any material with a bright, concrete surface harmonizes with them.

In addition to creating walls 1.8m/6ft high, low ones around the perimeter of a front garden are effective. Lay two or three courses of bricks and then one row of screen-block walling with concrete coping blocks on top. Around patios, increase this to two courses of screening blocks: ensure that the foundations are firm and strong.

They are also versatile enough to form surrounds for dustbins and sides of carports.

Concrete   Compacted hardcore

Reinforcing rod

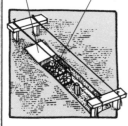

Pier

1. CREATE *foundations by digging a trench 30cm/1ft deep and 38cm/15in wide. Knock pegs into the base every 60cm/2ft to indicate the top of the concrete. Check that their tops are level. Fill the base with consolidated hardcore, then concrete.*

2. USE *specially-bought pier units as the ends. These enable blocks to be slotted into them. Use mortar to secure them to the foundations as well as to each other. Also, reinforce tall piers with metal rods and mortar.*

3. START *laying the blocks along the base, ensuring mortar does not get on the face side. Place mortar evenly over the ends and systematically butt one block against another. Regularly check that the bricks are being laid level and upright.*

WALLING IDEAS

Walls should be more than dividers between parts of a garden, or just around a garden's perimeter. Here are a few ideas:

• If your house is pebble-dashed and painted white, use breeze or concrete blocks to create a wall quickly. Foundations are needed, the same as used for brick walls. After construction and when the mortar has set, skim a thin layer of cement and sharp sand over the surface. When dry, apply another layer, at the same time adding 6mm/1/4in shingle. Add a coping and paint white.

• Old, second-hand bricks create superb ornamental walls, and to make them cover a large area, they do not have to be made into a solid wall. Create strong foundations, then lay the first course, leaving about a 7.5cm/3in gap between each brick. In the centre of each gap lay half-bricks, then a full one on top. Then, use full bricks to join these up, but again leaving about 7.5cm/3in between them. Continue to build up the wall to the desired height.

• Logs about 1.2m/4ft long and 15–20cm/6–8in wide create novel

LOW, DOUBLE WALLS

These are ideal for separating areas of the garden and to enable low, cascading plants to be grown. Ensure water can escape from the compost (insert pipes low down in the wall), but add plenty of moisture-retentive materials, such as peat, to the soil to prevent rapid drying in summer. Indeed, hot and dry summers can soon kill plants in raised walls: water the plants regularly.

'walls' for children's play areas. Bury their ends about 30cm/12in in soil and ram it tightly around their bases. Young children like to think of this as a fortress – and when the youngsters grow up the logs can be formed into log steps. They can also be used to enclose large areas of sand.

4. ENSURE *the ends fit snugly into the piers, so that they support each other. As an alternative to these piers, build brick ones about 23cm/9in square. They help screen-block walling to harmonize with other, nearby brickwork.*

5. BUILD *up the tiers of blocks, checking each one is level and vertical, as well as not bulging sideways. To produce a regular pattern, ensure the blocks are perfectly aligned vertically as well as horizontally. If the pattern is askew, they look a mess.*

6. FINISH *by cementing copings into place along the top of the wall. Also, cement coping on the piers. These both create a professional appearance and prevent deterioration from rain penetrating the joints and blocks, then freezing.*

DRY-STONE WALLS

❖

W HEN watching a craftsman constructing a dry-stone wall, the technique looks easy, but it requires skill and observation to select a suitable stone for a particular position. Both free-standing and retaining walls can be created: those used to retain soil have a slope (batter) while ordinary walling types are given an equal slope on both sides. Do not make them more than 1.2m/4ft high.

Stones can be obtained from garden centres, builders' yards, stone merchants and quarries. Many types can be used, granite or basalt being the hardest and most durable. It can be bought irregularly shaped or with regular, flat edges. Whatever the type of stone,

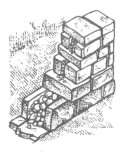

THE *key to success with dry-stone walls is firm foundations and to ensure water does not remain in the structure. Build up the sides, but allow some stones to cross the centre. These walls create wonderful opportunities to grow rock garden plants, especially if you do not have space for a rock garden.*

ensure its colour and texture harmonizes with the rest of your garden. About one tonne/2205lbs of rock is needed for every cubic metre of wall, and when buying it ensure the delivery charge is included in the price of the stone. A sound base is essential: dig out a trench, about twice the width of the expected top and 45cm/1½ft deep. Fill with rubble and thoroughly ram it into place. Lay several rows along the outside and fill between them with small stones. As the wall is built up, place large stones across the complete wall to tie the two sides together. Towards the top, use sandy soil in the centre to form pockets for plants. Finish by laying a coping of large, flat stones, with a slight tilt to one side.

1. DRY-STONE *walls are superb in rural areas. They can also be used in gardens to create retaining walls: to withstand the pressure of soil they are 'battered' or sloped. Mark out the wall's shape with a frame and strings.*

2. BUILD *up the wall from a firm base (see above). Lay a few courses of large stones and fill between them with small stones. Use extra large ones to cross the wall. Finish off at the top with coping stones.*

3. FILL *in behind the wall with coarse stones to ensure excess water rapidly drains away. Towards the top, use a layer of sandy topsoil to enable either grass to be sown or plants to be grown in the wall.*

RETAINING WALLS

❖

THESE create the opportunity to attractively and practically separate one level in a garden from another. Additionally, gardens on severe slopes can be made easier to maintain by building a series of retaining walls, producing terraces.

These walls — especially informal types — create the chance to grow plants. Select the type of wall to harmonize with the rest of your garden (examples of each are shown below).

The most destructive force to retaining walls is water, not soil mounded against them. It is therefore essential that provision is made to enable water to escape, either through open gaps left between stones in informal walls, and holes between the brickwork in formal types. Pipes can also be fitted into the structure.

CONSTRUCTING WALLS

When using bricks to construct formal retaining walls, choose water-resistant, engineering types and use a mortar mix of one part cement to three of soft sand. About every 90cm/3ft, leave gaps to allow water to escape.

The wall can be given a longer life by putting a waterproof membrane (such as polythene sheeting, although proprietary ones are available) between the wall and drainage material placed against it. But take care not to block the drainage holes.

Natural stone is not cemented together and therefore water can seep out. Even so, narrow pipe drains installed across the wall's base encourage rapid drainage.

Trailing plants help to soften the edges of the wall, as well as hold the bricks together.

FORMAL

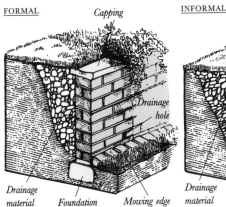

INFORMAL

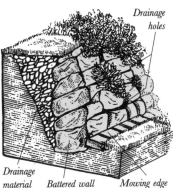

FORMAL, *vertical retaining walls must be kept relatively low (75cm/2¹/2ft) if they are to withstand the pressure of water as well as soil. Gaps in the wall's base are essential to enable water to escape.*

INFORMAL, *battered (leaning and angled backwards) retaining walls are stronger than vertical ones, but even these need a strong base and gaps to allow water to drain. Fill the back of the wall with clean rubble.*

FENCES

❖

FENCES should be pleasing to look at as well as functional. Their heights must suit their position and if needed to create a screen, should be solid. In towns and cities, rigidly outlined types such as close-boarded and over-lapped types are suitable, whereas in rural areas woven or wattle-hurdles are more sympathetic and have softer tones. Picket fencing also has rural characteristics and is easy to construct.

The range of fencing is wide, and in addition to those illustrated here a more recent type is ranch fencing: often seen in suburban gardens, painted white and with gaps left between the horizontal rails. A variation on this is to nail rails to both sides of posts, each overlapping the opposite one by about 12mm/1/2in.

In height, fences range from 90cm/3ft to 1.8m/6ft, but often 1.5m/5ft is a better choice. Most local planning regulations state that fences at the fronts of houses must not be more than 90cm/3ft, whereas in back gardens 1.8m/6ft is the limit.

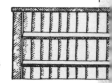
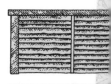

CLOSE-BOARDED *fences are constructed on site by first erecting posts, then arris rails.*

OVERLAPPING *boards nailed to framework create strong fences. Usually sold in panels.*

WOVEN *wood fences are sold in panels and later secured to strong posts.*

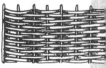

WATTLE *hurdling is inexpensive, sold in panels and has a soft, rustic nature.*

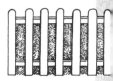

PICKET *fences have a country nature. Usually painted white, they have pointed or rounded tops.*

1. USE *string and pegs to mark the line of the fence. Ensure it is in the correct position and does not encroach on a neighbour's property. Allow for the width of posts when assessing its position.*

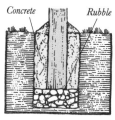

Concrete   Rubble

2. DIG *the first hole, 60cm/2ft deep and 30cm/12in square. Fill the base with 5cm/2in of rubble. Stand a post in it and check its top is 36mm/1 1/2in above a panel placed on a brick.*

3. PLACE *a panel on the ground and mark the next hole's position. Allow for space around the post when digging the hole. Check its height and concrete into position. Check that the post is upright.*

CONSTRUCTION AND MAINTENANCE

Whatever the type of fencing, it must be firmly secured to posts that have a long life-span. Here are a few ways to ensure fences remain in good condition:

• Check that posts are upright and secured in concrete. At the top of the concrete, smooth and angle it so that water runs off.

• Buy pressure-treated posts that have been impregnated with rot-resistance chemicals. For extra decay prevention, stand the bases overnight in cans filled with wood preservative.

• Do not allow the bases of panels to rest on the soil. Close-boarded fences should have an additional rail (gravel board) at their bases to fill the gap between the bases of vertical boards and soil. These are quickly replaced should they rot.

• Use only galvanized nails to secure fencing panels to posts. If nails rust, the whole panel might collapse and smash.

• Nail wooden caps to the tops of posts. Most are wooden, but some are formed of zinc. Alternatively, slant the tops of posts so that water runs off quickly.

REPAIRING BROKEN POSTS

If a fence post breaks, through old age or as a result of a storm, a new one can be easily fitted by using a special metal post base. These are hammered directly into the ground, but first place a wooden cap on top to prevent its top being damaged. Remove the cap, insert the post and secure its base. If not exposed to strong winds, low fences can be completely erected by using these spiked, metal bases.

• Regularly paint plain-wood fences with wood preservative. Coat both sides and ensure the paint reaches right into overlapping joints. Also, cover white picket and ranch-type fences with good quality paint.

• Regularly clear away soil and plants from the bases of fences as they encourage dampness and wood decay.

4. BEFORE *securing each panel to the posts, check that its base is about 5cm/2in above the soil – about the thickness of a brick. The bases of panels left resting on the ground soon deteriorate and rot away.*

5. SECURE *each panel firmly to posts by using 5cm/2in-long galvanized nails. For a 60cm/5ft high fence, four or five nails are needed at each end of a panel – the top and bottom – and then two in between.*

6. TO PREVENT *a post decaying through water entering its top, use two 36mm/1 1/2in-long galvanized nails to secure a capping to each post. These are readily available from suppliers of fences.*

CONSTRUCTING
A BOARDED FENCE

❖

UNLIKE panelled fencing that arrives in prefabricated lengths, usually 1.8m/6ft, and is then secured between posts, boarded fencing is constructed on site. First, holes are dug about 3m/10ft apart, posts positioned in them and arris rails inserted into slots in their sides. The posts are propped upright and held in position with supports while concrete is poured around them. When dry, the props are removed and erection of the feathered boards can begin. However, if the arris rails and posts need coating in wood preservative, now is the time to do it, when they can be readily reached with a brush.

GRAVEL BOARDS

The first part to be fitted is the gravel board. This is about 3m/10ft long, 15cm/6in deep and 18–25mm/³/₄–1in thick, and secured at the bases of fences to fill the gap between the feathered boards and soil. Its prime function is to prevent the main part of the fence rotting. Cleats (pieces of wood 2.5cm/1in square and the depth of the gravel board) are nailed to the sides of the posts and then the gravel board to them.

The main part of the fence is formed of feathered boards – these are tapered to one side. Cut them to the desired length, about 5cm/2in below the tops of the posts. These are then nailed to the arris rails. Use a notched gauge to ensure each feathered board overlaps its neighbour evenly, and use one nail at the top and another on the lower arris rail. Towards the end of each 3m/10ft section, adjust the overlapping spacings to ensure the boards fit evenly. Either fit protective caps to the tops of posts or cut their tops at an angle, so that water rapidly drains off.

Immediately after completion, coat the fence with a wood preservative. Repeat the coatings every year, forcing the preservative well into the wood. After a few years – and especially during dry, hot summers – the boards twist. Nail them back into position.

1. ARRIS *rails (horizontal bars on which vertical boards are nailed) often rot at their ends and fall out of their sockets. If this happens, use proprietary, rust-resistant brackets to replace them.*

2. SECURE *gravel boards to the bases of posts. These are essential to ensure vertical boards do not touch the soil, become damp and decay. It also improves the fence's appearance.*

3. NAIL *the feathered-edged boards to the arris rails. To ensure a uniform overlay, use a notched gauge to measure each board, top and bottom. Only one galvanized nail is needed at the top.*

WIRE-MESH FENCING

This fencing is also erected on site and the traditional form is the chain-link type, with bent wires that link with others and form a mesh. It is commonly sold in rolls – 10m/33ft, 25m/82ft and 50m/164ft long, and in heights from about 75cm/2¹/₂ft to 1.8m/6ft. As well, there is a range of mesh sizes, 36–50cm/1¹/₂–2in being about right for most gardens. Initially, this type of fencing appears cheaper than panel types of the same height, but it can be more expensive to install. This is because strong, firmly secured end posts are essential, so that wires can be strained between them. The mesh is then secured to the tensioned wires.

In addition to chain-link fencing there is the traditional chicken wire. This has been greatly improved for home gardens by a plastic coating. There are other plastic-coated wires in attractive patterns, in heights from 30cm/1ft to 1.2m/4ft – or more.

As well as forming fences, wire-mesh netting, when coiled into small, circular columns, supports climbing plants.

CONSTRUCTING A HA-HA

Also known as a haw-haw and sunken fence, it is a ditch that acts as a hidden fence, allowing uninterrupted views. The side towards the house usually has a slight slope, while the other one is vertical and lined in old stone walling to prevent crumbling.

It is said to have been used by French landscape designers in the seventeenth century and to have gained its name from people who came upon them suddenly and said Ah! Ah! It was introduced to Britain by Charles Bridgeman in the early eighteenth century to replace the 'unnaturalness' of walls. Lancelot 'Capability' Brown made them popular.

4. AT THE *base, rest each feathered-board on the gravel board and use one nail to secure it to the lower arris rail. Progress along the fence, but near to the next post adjust the spacings.*

5. POSTS *used for boarded fences are usually given sloping tops to enable rain to run off quickly. Alternatively, use wooden caps or pieces of zinc folded over the top and nailed to it.*

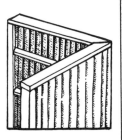

6. AS AN *added refinement, secure a strip of wood about 6cm/2¹/₂in wide and 18–25mm/³/₄–1in thick along the top of the fence. This protects the end grain on the feathered boards.*

GATES

—❖—

WELL-PROPORTIONED gates that harmonize with a garden and house enhance a property. Most gates are chosen for a combination of aesthetic and practical reasons, including keeping out wandering dogs, restraining your own pets and keeping children safe. Sometimes, their role is solely functional, perhaps to screen off a side entrance or to create a security barrier. Whatever the reason, there are many styles to choose from, and a nearly infinite range of sizes. The basic materials are metal and wood.

WOODEN GATES

Wood is a very adaptable material and can be formed into many styles, from solid-screen types to those with an open nature. Most are painted – usually white – but some are constructed in hardwoods that require only oiling or varnishing. Here are a few types of gate to consider:

• Picket fencing-type gates harmonize with similar style fencing

KISSING GATES

These have eye-appeal as well as romantic associations. They are unusual, with the gate hinged so that it swings between the two ends of a U-shaped recess. It ensures people passing through have to linger in a confined area while the gate swings back, perhaps leaving time for romantic dalliance!

as well as between two brick posts that mark the ends of a neat, relatively low hedge.

• Country gates, in softwood painted white or hardwood with a natural colour, are ideal for drives. Narrow ones for paths are also available. They look superb when used with post-and-rail fencing.

• Solid boarded gates – especially tall ones – must be firmly constructed and secured to strong hinges and posts as they are likely to be bufeted by wind. They have

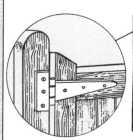 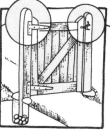 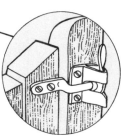

WOODEN *gates are popular but soon decay if not maintained properly. Long metal hinges are essential to ensure the gate is well secured. When fitting, first attach the hinge to the gate, then to the post.*

THE *stress points on wooden gates are the hinges, latches and where the wood is jointed. Rain, sun and freezing temperatures soon destroy a gate that is not well maintained – and prevent children swinging on it.*

SELF-CLOSING *latches are essential, especially if you have young children or a dog. Special springs – about 20cm/8in long – can be fitted to the hinge side to ensure that the gate closes and is secured by its latch.*

arched or flat tops and are available in planed softwood or hardwood.

• Ranch-style gates are essential for fences with a similar design. Occasionally, instead of constructing them with horizonal rails, these are put in vertically to create a contrast.

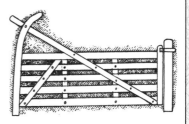

METAL GATES

Weather-resistant, wrought-iron gates have been used for many decades. These are made in single and double-gate forms and in a range of sizes. Most modern types are fitted with adjustable hinges to make fitting them easier.

There are many gates to choose from and, clearly, the more ornate their design the costlier they are. Ensure that the design harmonizes with its surrounds: avoid using highly ornate gates in relatively plain gardens.

• Tall gates with rounded tops are ideal for fitting into arches. Manufacturers produce these gates in many sizes, filling gaps from 75cm/2^1/2ft to 1.2m/4ft, but allow space around them for hinges and latches.

• Both single and double gates look superb when combined with brick walls. Their appearance can be complemented by fitting matching railings into the wall.

THE range of gates is wide, in both metal and wood. They are sold in a wide range of sizes to fill practically all positions. Most have a 'see-through' nature, but completely boarded types are available.

ANTI-THEFT HINGES

Modern wrought-iron gates usually have the peg parts of hinges built into them — top one pointing downwards, lower one upwards. When secured to the other part of the hinge (attached to a post or wall) this makes them theft-proof. Older types, however, often have the peg parts attached to the post. To ensure the gate is theft-proof, secure the lower peg upwards, top one downwards.

TRELLISES

❖

TRELLISES are essential to create support for climbers that twine naturally or have tendrils or leaf stalks that need something to which they can cling. These include flowering climbers such as clematis, Passion Flower and Sweet Peas, as well as the yellow coloured Golden-leaved Hop. Climbers that lean also need support, such as roses and the Winter-flowering Jasmine.

TYPES OF TRELLIS

These are traditionally made of wood, but plastic types are now widely available.

• Wooden trellises are formed of either square or diamond-shaped holes. The square-hole type is sold in sizes 1.8m/6ft high and widths such as 30cm/1ft, 60cm/2ft, 90cm/3ft, 1.2m/4ft and 1.8m/6ft. Each has an outer wooden framework, making it ideal for both fixing to walls and as free-standing units within a garden. This type is also available in fan-style units, about 1.8m/6ft high by 60cm/2ft at its widest point.

The diamond-shaped type is sold in a collapsed form and later expanded to cover areas 1.8m/6ft high and widths including 30cm/1ft, 45cm/1¹/₂ft, 60cm/2ft, 90cm/3ft and 1.2m/4ft. Because it is expandable, it does not have a firm surround and therefore needs to be nailed to a framework or directly on to a fence or wall.

• Rolls of plastic mesh are widely available, in many shapes and several colours. This does not have a rigid shape and must therefore be secured to a fence or other framework. It is relatively cheap to buy and can be adapted to fit most positions.

• Tubular, plastic-covered metal frameworks to form arches are sold in kit form.

JOINTED TRELLIS

Prefabricated, square-hole trelliswork invariably has cross-members nailed on top of vertical timbers. However, when making a trellis at home, the timbers can be let into one another by using cross-halving joints and creating trellises ideal as free-standing

1. POSITION *the trellis on a wall, so that its base is 23–30cm/9–12in above the ground. Use a spirit-level to ensure it is straight. Do not position the base of the trellis on the soil as it soon rots.*

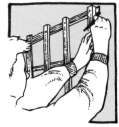

2. MARK *the exact position of the trellis on the wall to ensure it can be relocated in the same place later. While doing this, support the base on a box to ensure its position is constant.*

3. MARK *on the trellis the positions where it is to be drilled. Most trellises need to be secured to a wall in at least six places. At the same time, check that the brickwork is sound.*

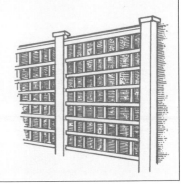

FREE-STANDING TRELLIS

Prefabricated, square-hole units can be formed into a free-standing trellis. But ensure they have a firm frame. Secure posts into the ground (see pages 30 and 31) and nail the trellis between them. This is an ideal way to separate one part of the garden from another. Use climbers to cover them.

units. However, do not use them against walls as they do not allow space for shoots to clamber behind them unless wooden spacers are used.

Use 2.5cm/1in square timber slats and cut half of them to the desired width of the trellis, the others to the depth. If the trellis is square, place all the timbers together, side by side, and secure them with adhesive tape. Use sufficient timber to create 18–23cm/7–9in squares. Use a long ruler to mark the wood 2.5cm/1in from both ends, then at equal spacings between, remembering to allow for the width of the timber at each position. Use a saw to cut

half-way through, then separate them and use a chisel to cut out the sawn areas. Then, slot the slats together, using a waterproof glue and 2.5cm/1in-long galvanized nails to secure the trellis.

SCREEN-COVERING CLEMATIS

- Clematis flammula:
Sweetly-scented, small, white flowers during mid and late summer.
- Clematis macropetala:
Light and dark blue, bell-shaped flowers during early summer.

4. PLACE *the trellis on several pieces of wood and use a drill to form holes in the wood. Do not force the drill through the timber. Rather, let it pass gently through the wood.*

5. RELOCATE *the trellis on the wall, place a long, thick nail in each hole and knock with a hammer. This will mark the surface of the wall so that the drilling positions are clearly marked.*

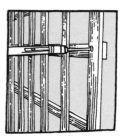

6. REMOVE *the trellis and use a masonry drill to make holes in the wall. Insert wall-fixing plugs, relocate the trellis and initially only partly tighten the screws. Later, tighten them fully.*

CARPORTS

❖

THESE are relatively new in concept and a reflection of man's passion for motoring and protecting his car. Garages are a natural and logical transition from coach-houses, but carports are more a mid-century, inexpensive expediency to protect cars from the rain – and therefore rust.

Most are attached to house walls, with both ends directly accessible and the fourth side partially screened, perhaps by brick-work, wood or screen-block walling. However, instead of aligning it alongside a house or existing garage, position it at a right-angle and use one side – perhaps bricked – to form a courtyard.

Firm, all-weather surfaces are essential for cars and these are described earlier, but an alternative includes laying large paving slabs for the car's wheels to run upon, and creating a gravel surface between them. The advantage of gravel is that if a car drips oil, the contaminated area can be removed and quickly replaced with fresh chippings.

PLANNING

Do not ignore the planning stage and apply for – should it be necessary – permission from local authorities. Planning officers are very helpful and a visit or phone call could save you money and time. If permission is needed, part of this depends on your house's building line.

CONSTRUCTION

Methods vary widely, with supports formed of brick pillars, wood or tubular metal. Roofing is frequently made of corrugated, transparent sheeting, overlapping several corrugations and directing water into guttering to drain it into a water-barrel or a sump dug in a garden. Eventually, sunlight deteriorates the roofing material.

Some carports have a secondary and more ornate roof secured to the lower sides of the roofing bars, helping to create a structure more harmonious with its surroundings. Before deciding on your carport's construction, inspect as many as you can and talk to the owners

ENSURE *the design and constructional materials harmonize with the house. Make it appear part of a garden's overall design, not something added later. Walls along parts of the sides provide extra protection, but ensure they do not create a wind-tunnel. Also, make sure the structure complies with local building regulations.*

CARPORTS *made of wood have a softer outline and texture than those of brick and soon become part of the garden. If constructed as part of a shed or existing garage, use the same materials and a similar design. Ensure there is provision for water drainage from the roof. Use water-butts, but ensure they are covered to prevent leaves entering.*

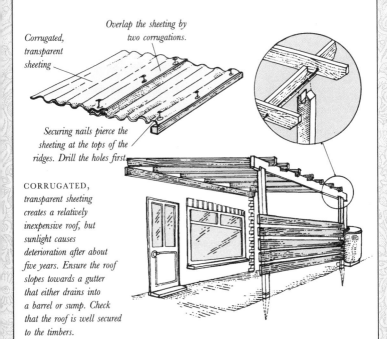

Corrugated, transparent sheeting

Overlap the sheeting by two corrugations.

Securing nails pierce the sheeting at the tops of the ridges. Drill the holes first.

CORRUGATED, *transparent sheeting creates a relatively inexpensive roof, but sunlight causes deterioration after about five years. Ensure the roof slopes towards a gutter that either drains into a barrel or sump. Check that the roof is well secured to the timbers.*

about construction as well as as the ease of maintenance.

Screen-block walling – perhaps combined with a brick wall – offers an easy way to create extra protection and to prevent rain lashing on the sides of cars.

BLENDING

Use shrubs, climbers and wall-shrubs to soften the construction's outline and to harmonize it with the garden. Positioning yellow-leaved, narrow conifers on either side of the entrance is useful when negotiating it at night. Avoid setting climbing or rambling roses up the supports as their thorns are certain to tear clothing. More importantly, however, long stems on rambling roses may blow into your face. Large-leaved ivies – such as the variegated Persian Ivy, *Hedera colchica* 'Dentata Variegata' – soon soften the lines of supports and the fronts of roofs.

TIMBER AND
BRICK PERGOLAS

TIMBER is a very adaptable and versatile material: when planed it has a formality that especially harmonizes with modern architecture, while if roughly sawn and painted with a dark preservative it blends with old, white-painted cottages.

Pergolas were known in antiquity, in Egypt, and later in Italy. Initially they simply supported plants, but later became architectural features. During the Italian Renaissance they started to spread throughout Europe.

Nowadays, formal types are formed with brick or wood supports, but invariably the cross-members are timber. Clearly, those made from wood are cheaper and quicker to erect than ones created with brick or stone pillars. Foundations for both brick and stone pillars must be sound, especially on clay soil, and involve digging footings 60cm/2ft deep.

Indeed, the life expectancy of brick pillars depends on the footings and the accuracy in subsequent construction. Securing cross timbers to them is a matter of cementing bolts or threaded rods to the tops or, with tall, narrow columns, a reinforcing rod that extends from the foundations to the top and is secured by a nut.

Cross-halving joints are used to join and hold timbers together. This involves measuring the width of the area to be cut and using a set-square to enscribe around the timber. Mark the depth of the cut. Hold the timber firm and use a tenon saw to cut the sides. Also, make several cuts to the same depth in the centre, depending on the area to be removed. Turn the timber on its side and use a chisel to cut out the piece that will enable another timber to be let into it. Ensure it fits comfortably, but not too tightly, as, if the wood swells, the timber may split.

BRICK PILLARS

Pillars constructed of bricks or stone create distinctive and elegant pergolas. Columns, about 35cm/14in or 45cm/18in square, are needed, their thickness and proportions depending on the beams and the pergola's extent. The beams are secured to the tops of pillars either by masonry bolts or threaded metal rods secured with concrete in the columns and held with nuts.

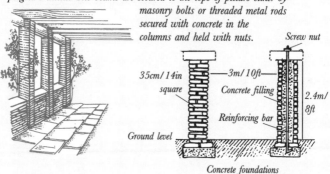

Screw nut

35cm/14in
square

—3m/10ft—

Concrete filling

2.4m/8ft

Reinforcing bar

Ground level

Concrete foundations

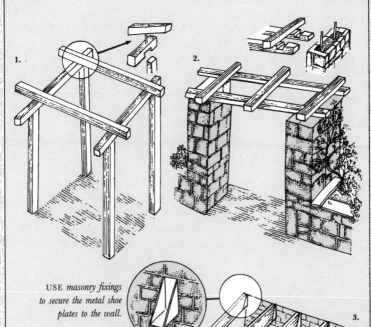

1.

2.

USE *masonry fixings to secure the metal shoe plates to the wall.*

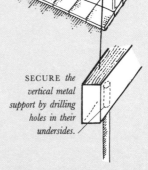

3.

PLANED TIMBER *creates a formal pergola and, because the wood is square or rectangular, it is relatively easy to make any joints that are required. To ensure the wood's long life, buy timber that has been treated with preservatives. Some are pressure-treated and this ensures even longer life. The range of designs is wide and includes free-standing types as well as those secured to wall or brick supports.*

1. CEMENT *10cm/4in-square timbers 45–60cm/1^1/2–2ft into the ground and use a spirit-level to ensure their tops are all the same height. Use two pieces of 10cm/4in-square (or 7.5cm/3in x 10cm/4in) timber. Use cross-halving joints to recess the cross timbers into the uprights. When they are in place, drill 12mm/^{1}/2in holes through the cross-timbers and slightly into the vertical posts, then secure with coach bolts.*

2. SECURE *the timbers by cementing bolts or threaded rods to the tops of the brickwork. When all the timbers have been jointed, drill holes in them, place on top and secure with washers and nuts.*

SECURE *the vertical metal support by drilling holes in their undersides.*

3. EXISTING *walls can provide support for one side of a pergola. Use metal wall shoes to hold them, with tubular, metal supports at the other side. Fix them firmly in concrete blocks in the ground.*

RUSTIC PERGOLAS

❖

THESE have an aged, rural and timeless quality that endears them to many gardeners. They are perfect companions for many climbers, especially roses, honeysuckle and clematis, and soon blend in with the rest of a garden.

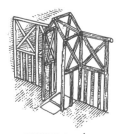

RUSTIC *pergolas are superb for providing places for climbers.*

Timber yards sell (or can order for you) rustic poles, usually formed of larch or pine and with their bark still attached. Sometimes this is removed (known as dressed) and the poles treated with a wood preservative. Alternatively, after construction they are coated in varnish. Dressed poles have a more clinical and modern nature than those with their bark left in place, and may better suit the style of your garden. But do not use dressed poles for large pergolas, as they can be a shock to the eye.

If you are considering using the pergola as an architectural feature, rather than primarily to support plants, dressed poles are worth considering.

Strong construction is essential. Pickling the bases of poles overnight in wood preservative is vital. First, however, remove bark from the lower 60cm/2ft and ensure that the preservative is plant-friendly and will not later damage plants.

If possible, inspect the poles before buying to ensure they are sound and straight. Additionally, each pole must be relatively uniform in width, and all the poles should be of an even diameter, if possible. This makes jointing them much easier and creates a better-looking pergola.

Vertical poles need to be about 3m/10ft long, enabling 45–60cm/1½–2ft to be buried in the ground. Horizontal poles should be selected for their uniform thickness and be 3.6–4.5m/12–15ft long. It is pointless trying to buy extra long horizontal poles.

ONE *method to join oblique timbers to vertical or horizontal ones is to cut their ends at an angle and to use galvanized nails to joint them. To prevent wood splitting, first drill the oblique timber.*

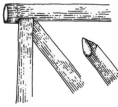

ANOTHER *way to join oblique timbers is to cut both sides of the end, so that it fits snugly into the angle of vertical and horizontal timbers. Drill the end before securing it with galvanized nails.*

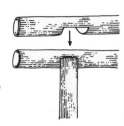

TO SECURE *horizontal rustic poles to vertical supports, make a halving joint in the cross member, so that the upright fits snugly but does not strain and split it. Drill the horizontal timber, then nail together.*

JOINTING AND NAILING

Joints to use when securing poles together are illustrated below. Ensure the joints fit snugly and use galvanized nails. Their lengths must be at least the thickness of the first pole and two-thirds through the second one. Drill holes in the first pole so that the nail fits tightly. And while knocking in each nail, ask a companion to hold the head of a club- or sledge-hammer on the opposite side: this ensures the nail is firmly secured as well as preventing the structure from being badly shaken.

When assessing the widths of arches, make them at least 90cm/ 3ft wider than the path. This ensures that climbers with prickly thorns will not cause damage.

HONEYSUCKLES

Honeysuckles are ideal for covering pergolas and trellises. Lonicera periclymenum *'Belgica' flowers during early summer (purple-red and yellow), while L. p. 'Serotina' has red-dish-purple and creamy-white flowers from mid to late summer.*

VARIED DESIGNS

Rustic poles are adaptable and many differently shaped pergolas and arches can be created. Here are a few designs: arches, either across paths or as features in lawns to support roses and other climbers. Additionally, these poles are ideal for creating free-standing trellises to separate one part of a garden from another. Check trellises regularly to ensure they are safe, and it is not just plants that are holding them up.

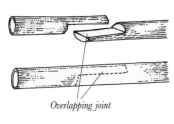

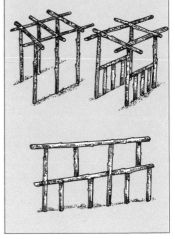

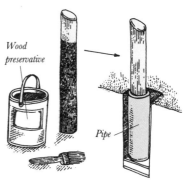

Overlapping joint

WHERE *long pergolas are needed it is necessary to join timbers. Choose timbers of equal thickness and measure about 25cm/10in from both of their ends. Cut halfway through and then down the centre, so that they can be painted with a preservative and secured with galvanized nails.*

Wood preservative

Pipe

REMOVE *bark and immerse the end in preservative overnight. Further protect the end when buried by standing it in a drainage pipe, then filling with cement.*

ROCK GARDENS
❖

HESE create the opportunity to grow a large number of small, often delicate, plants in a restricted area. Primarily, rock gardens are for alpine plants but others, including miniature conifers, blend with the area and create variations in height.

When selecting a site, it must be well-drained and away from overhanging trees that create shade and drip plant-rotting water in winter. Additionally, avoid positions that are in extremely hot sun continuously throughout the day.

SITE PREPARATIONS
Rock gardens are ideally built on slight slopes, although artificial mounds can be created within a garden. Alternatively, if the area is flat and you do not want the expense of buying in topsoil, dig a path around the proposed area to a depth of 30–45cm/1–1½ft and use this soil to create a mound. First, however, remove topsoil from both areas and use drains to ensure that the paths will not become flooded in winter.

Good drainage is essential with all rock gardens, so when artificially creating one, first form a 23–30cm/9–12in-thick base of clean rubble. Then, begin to create the mound.

When buying in topsoil, ensure it is free from perennial weeds. Once Couch Grass or Horsetail gets into a rock garden it is practically impossible to remove it other than by dismantling the complete area and either sifting the soil or buying in fresh.

In addition, check that the soil is free from pests, such as wireworms and cockchafer grubs.

SCREE BEDS

In Nature, these are found at the bases of groups of rocks, where constant weathering has broken them down into small pieces. In gardens, this theme can be then continued or, in small gardens, made a feature on its own. Plant it with small alpines.

GARDENS *with slopes are ideal places for the construction of rock gardens. This both expands the range of plants that can be grown in a garden and deals with a slope that otherwise might be difficult to cultivate.*

MOUNDS *of topsoil – placed on a well-drained base – form picturesque free-standing rock gardens that can be combined with a garden pond. It should appear to be a natural outcrop of rocks.*

A POSITION *in an angle of two walls is another possibility for a small rock garden. A scree-bed around it – or a shingle path – makes it even more natural. Indeed, all rock gardens must appear to be natural.*

1. DIG *the base about 45cm/1¹/2ft deep. Fill with 23-30cm/9-12in of clean rubble. Use topsoil to create a 1.2m/4ft high mound, then start by adding rocks at the edge.*

2. ROCK *gardens must appear to be natural outcrops of rocks. All rocks should tilt slightly backwards, giving the impression of an extension of the natural strata. If possible use local stones.*

3. LAY *the rocks with about one-third buried, so that they appear to tilt out of the ground. This both looks natural and ensures that rainwater trickles back and around the roots of plants.*

CONSTRUCTION

The range of possible stone is wide, but it is preferable to use local materials as they blend best with the surroundings. As an estimate of the amount of stone needed, a rock garden 3m/10ft by 5.4m/18ft will need about 2 tonnes/4410lb of stone, in a range of sizes.

Take care not to use rock quarried from areas of natural beauty which therefore diminishes the environment. Also, do not use limestone in city areas: an acid atmosphere makes it remain white and unweathered.

Start laying rocks at the base of the mound, burying at least one-third and giving each stone a slight tilt backwards. It is essential to create a natural appearance, as if the stones are in a strata and just appearing out of the ground. When the first row is in position, put the second one in place. However, avoid creating a tiered wedding cake with strict lines and distances between the rows. Indeed, at one side they could nearly meet.

Ensure each stone is firm and can, if necessary, be stood upon. Spread a mixture of topsoil, peat and grit over the soil and firm it around the rocks. After setting the plants in position, spread a 12mm/¹/2in layer of 6mm/¹/4in rock chippings over the surface to keep the soil moist and roots cool. Use small, limestone chippings for lime-loving plants, and granite or gravel for others.

DRY-STONE WALLS

If you are unable to have a rock garden, a dry-stone wall can create an alternative home. Select cascading plants for the top and set small plants in gaps between the stones. As well as being attractive, the roots of plants help to bind the wall together.

MAKING A POND
WITH A LINER

❖

FLEXIBLE pond liners are made either from polythene, PVC (which can be reinforced with nylon) or butyl rubber, which is the most expensive but invariably longest wearing.

FLEXIBLE *liners are an ideal way to create garden ponds: they are adaptable, have a long life and are relatively quick to install. Create neat edges from edging bricks, crazy-paving or small slabs.*

The pond's size is important; if too shallow, it freezes in winter and becomes too hot in summer. Also, a deep pond enables a wider range of plants to be grown than a shallow one.

There is an optimum area needed to support fish. For example, ten small fish need to have a surface area of at least 1.8 square metres (about 20 square feet). Because they grow – and breed – make the pond much larger than you initially envisage. If there are too many fish in a pond the oxygen is depleted, especially in summer when water is relatively warm.

Assess the size of liner you need by measuring the width and adding twice the depth plus about 90cm/ 3ft. It is better to be generous with its size than later to find it is too small! Liners can also be used for raised ponds. Double-check the measurements and, if necessary, drape a piece of soft rope in the hole and up the sides, then measure it.

Both informal and formal outlined ponds can be made from flexible liners: if the former, use a hosepipe to create its outline and position. Dig out the area, removing turf (if situated in a lawn), as well as from 30cm/12in around it. This creates space for edging strips.

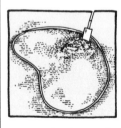

1. USE *a hosepipe to mark the pool's position and shape on the lawn – it can be altered many times until a pleasing design is found. Then, use a spade to cut the shape on the grass, following the inside edge of the hosepipe.*

2. FIRST *remove the grass, then the topsoil and later subsoil, keeping them separate. Create a 'shelf' around the side, about 23cm/9in from the surface. Then, dig deeper to form the base, 45–60cm/1½–2ft below the surface.*

3. IF THE *pond is dug out of a lawn, also remove turf to 5cm/2in deep from area 30cm/12in around it. Use a spirit-level on top of a long, evenly-thick board to check that the sides are level. If necessary, dig down on one side.*

Keep the turf separate (it may be useful for re-turfing bare patches elsewhere), as well as the topsoil and subsoil. Create a 23cm/9in wide shelf about the same distance from the surface, then dig the base at least 23cm/9in deeper. This is the minimum depth: one 75–90cm/2½–3ft in parts is better, but not essential. Koi carp, however, need deeper water, preferably about 1.5m/5ft, to keep them warm during winter.

After the pond area has been dug out, use a spirit-level on a long board to ensure the sides are at the same height.

Remove stones protruding from the sides, then cover the base and sides with soft sand. If the area is exceptionally stony, also line the pond with polythene sheeting.

Place the liner in position and temporarily secure its sides with bricks. Gently trickle water on to the liner and regularly ease back the bricks. Create folds in the liner as it assumes the pond's shape. Then, fold back the liner at the top and use mortar to secure a neat and attractive edging on top of it.

INFORMAL EDGES

Camouflaging the edges of rural ponds is essential. If left with the liner emerging at the edges it diminishes its attractiveness. Also, sunlight eventually deteriorates the liner.

After filling the pond and ensuring its edges are at the same height, fold back the liner and cut off, leaving a 23–30cm/ 9–12in overlap. Then, lay plastic-covered chicken-wire over it, securing it to the ground about 23cm/9in from the pond with hooks made from stiff wire (old metal coat-hangers are ideal when cut into 25cm/10in lengths and bent to form a U-shape). Turves can then be laid on top – the wire keeps them in position until knitted together. Alternatively, lay strips of old carpet and place either soil or turf on top. Hold the carpeting in place with pieces of bent wire. When cutting grass around a pond, take care that the clippings do not fall into the water.

4. REMOVE *sharp protrusions from the sides and base and lay soft sand on them. This is vital, as the weight of water against a sharp stone soon punctures liners. Then, spread the liner across the hole and place bricks on its edges.*

5. GENTLY *allow water to trickle into the hole and continually ease off the bricks so that the liner becomes moulded to the shape of the hole. If there are folds in the liner, ensure these are neat and unobtrusive.*

6. CUT *off excess liner, leaving a 10–15cm/4–6in overlap around the edge. Place edging bricks on top, bedded on a mixture of one part cement and three of soft sand. They should overhang the pool by about 5cm/2in to cloak the liner.*

MAKING A POND
WITH A PRE-CAST SHELL
❖

EARLY shells were made of metal pressed into the desired shape. Nowadays, however, they are formed of glass-fibre, a composite material consisting of glass fibres in a resin.

Installing symmetrical pools is much easier than those with an irregular outline. Assessing the area for a round pond is detailed below, while for others it is basically a

CIRCULAR, *pre-cast shells create distinctive ponds in formal settings and are ideal for positioning at the junctions of paths. A central fountain or statue completes the design.*

stones at the other. Use a builder's spirit-level on top of a long, straight board to assess levels. It may be necessary to fill the shell with water and to empty it several times until the levels are right.

Creating an edging that harmonizes with the garden and other features is important and, whatever the materials, they should overlap the edge by about 5cm/2in. Lay

matter of trial and error until the shell fits snugly and evenly on the base of the hole. All shelves must also fit. By sprinkling soft sand over all the surfaces, its fitting can be judged by the impression the shell makes on it.

It is essential that the shell is level in all directions. If not, when filled with water there will be a noticeable gap at one end or water lapping over the edging

them on a bed of mortar formed from one part Portland cement and three of soft sand. And to ensure they do not topple into the water when their ends are stood upon, make the edging 30–45cm/12–18in wide.

Formal edging bricks suit round ponds, creating a symmetrical outline, whereas irregularly-shaped edgings are better around informally-shaped ponds.

1. SELECT *the area where the shell is to be installed, then invert it and mark around the outside. Preferably, the area should be level: if not, the soil at one side must be carefully excavated.*

2. REMOVE *the turf to a depth of 5cm/2in all over the area. Measure in from the edge and use pegs to mark the first shelf. Excavate the area and then mark the following level, again digging out and removing the soil.*

3. SPRINKLE *soft sand on the shelves and base, then place the shell in the hole. The shell will leave an impression on the base and the amount of sand can be increased or removed until it fits snugly in all places.*

VARIETY OF SHAPES

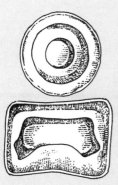

The range of shell shapes and sizes is wide and it is well worth consulting several water-gardening catalogues before making a decision. Round, symmetrically-shaped pools are easier than irregular ones to install but invariably have a clinical, formal outline.

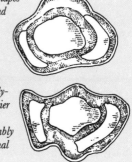

PONDS AND ROCK GARDENS

Ponds formed from shells are easily combined with rock gardens to create an even more spectacular display. In such situations, edging stones around the shell are only needed on one or two sides, the rock garden merging with it on the others.

Allow some large rock garden stones to slightly overlap the pond's edge, to soften and camouflage its outline and to prevent soil spilling into the water. A piece of wire-netting, slightly buried, helps to keep the soil stable and in place until the roots of plants are well established.

Use trailing plants to further soften the edges. Alternatively, if space allows, plant a prostrate conifer with colourful leaves to create colour throughout the year. Consider *Juniperus communis* 'Depressa Aurea' (golden-yellow foliage) with a 1.2m/4ft spread. Use such plants with care as they may eventually dominate a small pond. Nevertheless, plants are essential around the edges.

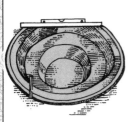

4. PLACE *a spirit-level across the shell to check its levels. Now is the time to make further alterations and to ensure the sides are at the same height. If the levels are wrong it will not look right when filled with water.*

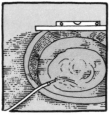

5. GENTLY *fill the shell with water. At the same time, continue to check the levels as sometimes the weight of water can cause settlement. If severe, pump out and adjust the amount of soft sand.*

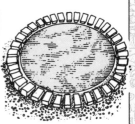

6. WHEN *filled, lay ornamental edging blocks around the side so that they protrude about 5cm/2in over the water's edge. Use a mortar mix of one part cement and three of soft sand to set them in place.*

MAKING A
CONCRETE POND
❖

APART from using puddled clay, concrete is perhaps the traditional method to create a garden pond. It has great strength, but is vulnerable to movement in soils, especially those formed mainly of clay. Therefore, unless properly and strongly constructed, concrete ponds eventually can be a disappointment. However, even if leaks do occur, there are proprietary sealants and paints that can be used. And even if these are not practical, the entire pond can be sealed with a flexible liner.

CONCRETE *pools, if well constructed and on a firm base, last for many years. Most have a rigid outline and therefore need to be positioned in a formal setting.*

The construction of a concrete pool is outlined below: for small ponds the thickness of concrete need be only 10cm/4in, but for large ones 15cm/6in is better, with a thicker, hardcore base.

Reinforcing wire, positioned half-way through the thickness of concrete, creates extra strength and is essential if the ground is mainly formed of clay. When positioning the reinforcing in the base, ensure the ends are bent to protrude 15–20cm/6–8in up the sides and about 5cm/2in in from the edges. After the base is set and before forming the shuttering for the edges, install reinforcing in the sides. When pouring concrete into the sides, ensure that this action is continuous and that no part is allowed to dry before more concrete is added. Long breaks between pouring the concrete encourage weakness later. Use a stick to push down the concrete to remove air pockets, which if left also cause weakness.

1. REMOVE *grass from the area and 30–45cm/ 1–1½ft around it. Then, mark out the pond with pegs (their tops about 7.5cm/3in above the surface) and use a builder's spirit-level to check they are level.*

2. DIG *out the area. As digging progresses, create shelves. Remember to remove soil 10–15cm/4–6in deeper – and 20–30cm/ 8–12in more in width – to allow for the thickness of concrete all around.*

3. LAY *5cm/2in of hardcore in the base. Then, 5cm/2in of concrete and a layer of reinforcing wire (bend up the ends). Add a further 5cm/2in thick layer of concrete. Tamp down the surface to remove air.*

CONCRETE MIXES

It is a mistake to think that increasing the amount of Portland cement in proportion to the sharp sand and aggregates makes the pool better or even stronger. It could, if taken to extremes, make it very brittle and prone to crack. To create concrete that is strong enough to withstand the pressure of water, use a mixture of 1 part Portland cement, 2½ parts sharp sand and 3½ parts of 20mm aggregate. Alternatively, use a mixture of 1 part Portland cement and 5 parts combined aggregate.

DANGEROUS CHEMICALS

Toxic chemicals within the concrete need to be leached before finally filling and introducing plants and fish. Normally, the pool must be filled and emptied four or five times. Alternatively, treat the surface with a proprietary sealant. Then, fill with water, allowing it to remain in the pond according to the manufacturer's instructions. Only when the water is clean add the plants and fish. Fish are highly sensitive and soon die if toxic chemicals are still present in the concrete.

RAISED PONDS

Ponds that rise above ground level create unusual features on patios. They do, however, need strong construction as even a small pond can hold a couple of tonnes/tons of water. Also, raised ponds are more likely to freeze during severe winter weather than those in the ground. Apart from being a hazard to fish, the ice tends to push the walls outwards and cause cracks. Therefore, in cold winters be prepared to use a water-heater.

Strong brickwork is essential, at least 23cm/9in thick and preferably 30cm/12in for large ponds. Use a flexible liner to create a waterproof membrane, tucking the edge over the top layer

of bricks and then using mortar to secure coping bricks or slabs in place.

4. WHEN *the base can be stood on, erect reinforcing wire 5cm/2in in from the sides. Secure this to the other wire. Then, erect shuttering that leaves a 10-15cm/4-6in gap. Pour concrete into the sides.*

5. WHEN *the concrete has hardened, carefully remove the shuttering. Cover all surfaces with a slurry of sharp sand and cement. When set hard, fill the pond with water several times to remove toxic chemicals.*

6. PLACE *edging slabs all the way around the pond's edge: ensure that they slightly overhang the edge and hide the tops of the sides. Wide slabs are better than narrow ones. Cement them into position.*

MAKING A WATERFALL

❖

WATERFALLS introduce a fascinating dimension to water gardens, producing a visually exciting and ever-changing scene. As well, the sound of water splashing from one level to another emphasizes its presence, as well as helping to oxygenate the pools and prevent stagnation.

Apart from using concrete, there are two basic methods used to create a series of waterfalls. Glass-fibre cascade units are available in a variety of sizes and shapes, and these can be secured on a firm bed of sand to form a series of small ponds and cascades. Alternatively, a series of waterfalls can be made from either one large sheet of flexible liner or several small pieces.

A slightly curving or meandering flight of waterfalls is better than a straight one, which neither looks natural nor creates any mystery. Ensure the lip of each waterfall is level, so that water cascades evenly over the full width.

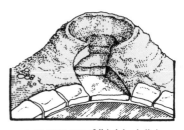

1. IF THE *waterfall is being built in conjunction with a pond, use excavated soil to create a mound. However, do not reuse clay where plants are to be grown. Dig out the top area to form a small pool and cut steps to channel water to the pond.*

2. USE *a flexible liner to create the top pool and watercourses. Either one large sheet can be used, or start from the bottom and lay several. They must overlap at the waterfalls. Each pool should have a slight tilt to its rear to ensure it retains water.*

3. SELECT *rectangular stones to create the edge of each waterfall. Cement these securely in place and to one another with a mortar mix of one part cement and three of soft sand. Their size and shape fundamentally influences the type of waterfall.*

LIGHTING A POND

Lighting pools, waterfalls, fountains and statuary brings gardens alive during summer evenings. Submersible lights can be used to highlight fish and fountains, while others float on the surface.

Most lights above ground are available in spot or flood modes. They are usually powered by electricity from a mains supply; low-powered systems with a transformer installed between the mains supply and the lights are available. Engage a competent electrician for installation.

INSTALLING A PUMP

Submersible pumps are essential to continually top up the pool at the apex of waterfalls. The size of pump depends on the height the top pool is above the main pond, as well as the widths of the waterfalls. A pump with a capacity of 1364 litres/300 gallons of water an hour is needed to create a continuous flow of water about 15cm/6in wide. A pump's output diminishes with the increasing height it is expected to pump water. Ensure the pump is installed to the highest electrical safety standards.

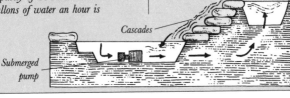

Cascades

Submerged pump

TYPES OF PUMPS

There are two main types of pumps used to create flows of water down waterfalls:

• <u>Submersible pumps</u> are entirely submerged and designed to operate silently and safely. And because they function from within a pond there is no need to build a pump chamber somewhere on the site to house them.

Installation is easy, the electrical cable being connected to a mains electricity supply through a waterproof connector situated in a small, dry chamber, perhaps under a paving stone. This allows the pump to be removed easily and quickly. All electrical connections must be earthed and, preferably, have a power-breaker device within the circuit to cut off instantly the electricity supply should there be a malfunction.

The range of pumps is wide and their power is measured in the litres/gallons of water they pump in an hour. The output required is influenced by the height the pump has to force the water and the widths of the cascades. For example, a pump with an output of 3182 litres/700 gallons when lifting water 90cm/3ft will only raise 1591 litres/350 gallons to 3m/10ft high. Also, to create a continuous trickle of water about 15cm/6in wide requires a flow of about 1364 litres/300 gallons an hour. Consult a specialist pump supplier or manufacturer before deciding on the type and size you need.

Filters are incorporated in the pumps and these must be regularly cleaned, according to the manufacturer's instructions. When not in use – usually from autumn to spring – remove the pump, service and store in a dry shed.

• <u>Surface pumps</u> are usually more powerful than submersible types and generally preferred when water has to be raised more than 3m/10ft. Also, if several fountains and a waterfall are required, a surface type is essential.

They have to be housed in a dry, well-ventilated chamber and tubes carrying the water must be relatively large to reduce friction. The pump can be positioned anywhere from below the level of the main pond to the top waterfall, but keep the pipe lengths as short as possible.

MAKING BENCHES AND TABLES

❖

GARDENING should not just be a continual round of mowing lawns, hoeing borders and turning over compost heaps; it ought also to be an area of relaxation and enjoyment. Benches therefore need to be sited where they offer a good view of a garden, while chairs and tables positioned on patios and terraces create an outdoor living area.

The range of ready-made garden furniture is extensive and in many materials, including reconstituted stone, marble, wrought iron, planed wood, tree-logs cut in strips, and strong plastic. In addition, many chairs and tables can be made or quickly assembled from kits sold in garden centres and do-it-yourself stores.

MAKING YOUR OWN

Personalizing your garden with furniture constructed yourself is very pleasing and satisfying. Here are a few ideas:

• Thick tree trunks cut into 75cm/2¹/₂ft lengths with their bases set 30cm/12in in the ground create a toadstool-like effect, ideal for woodland areas.

• Timber yards sometimes have large, 5–7.5cm/2–3in-thick sections of trees that are ideal to turn into benches and tables for rustic positions. Use thick logs to support them. Secure them together with long nails. Drill the top with several holes (so that nails fit tightly) and hammer them into the upright logs.

• If you are building a retaining or privacy wall along the edge of a patio or terrace, consider incorporating a bench into it. A wooden framework can be fitted later by using masonry fixings. Alternatively, leave a brick surface and make cushions to soften and cover the top.

• Wheeled patio loungers are readily available from shops, but they also can be made from wood. Basically, they are a framework, 1.8m/6ft by 75cm/2¹/₂ft, supported by two 20cm/8in wheels at one end and legs at the other. Cushions are also needed.

1. THIS *bench can be easily made at home from bricks and timber. First, form a strong brick base, 1.2-1.8m/4–6ft long, 60cm/2ft deep and 30–38cm/12–15in high (four or five courses of bricks).*

2. CUT *the sides from 18mm/³/4in-thick plywood (width and height 60cm/24in). Shape them (see above) and make 10cm/4in by 2.5cm/1in slots to accept the ends of the wooden cross members.*

3. SECURE *four, 15cm/6in long, 5cm/2in square pegs to the cross members to hold the frame within the brickwork. Use glue and wedges to secure the cross members to the sides. Then, add the seat struts.*

HOME-MADE BENCHES

Benches are easily made, such as simple ones consisting of planks of wood, concrete beams or slabs of marble secured to brick, concrete or wood bases. Junk yards and demolition sites often have materials that can be re-cycled for use in gardens. Old wooden railway sleepers create benches with a rustic appeal and look even better when harmonized with shrubs, such as the evergreen, small-leaved, Edging Box to create backs and sides.

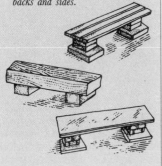

• Large slabs of reconstituted stone are readily available and, when placed on ornamental supports, create benches and tables. It is also possible to make your own from concrete. Create a mould 1.2–1.5m/4–5ft long and 30–60cm/1–2ft wide so that concrete can be poured in to a thickness of 7.5cm/3in. Form a 36mm/1¹/₂in-thick layer of a mixture of 1 part Portland cement, 2 parts sharp sand and 3 parts 20mm aggregate. Then, place several reinforcing metal rods on the mixture and top up to the surface with further concrete. Vibrate and tamp the mixture to remove air bubbles. Allow to harden for a couple of weeks before moving and using.

• Square or rectangular pre-cast paving slabs can, together with a brick base, be turned into permanent seats or tables. Screen-block wall can also be used to create a base. Although dirt may collect under this construction, it can be remove with a hosepipe and a stiff jet of water. However, be sure that they will blend in with the style of the patio or terrace.

WROUGHT-IRON *benches in the mid-nineteenth century were much lighter than the cast-iron types of a similar size, and therefore much easier to move.*

DURING *the 1970s and 80s, wooden garden swings from Finland became very popular – and were great fun.*

STRONG *garden tables are essential when dining outdoors. Some are made of wood (as shown here); others of metal.*

MAKING A BARBEQUE

DINING out-doors on a patio or terrace need not be a continual rush from a kitchen, carrying trays of food. Instead, food can be cooked outdoors on a barbeque. Proprietary ones are readily available, as well as mobile types, but they are also easily made from bricks. Most barbeques are cemented together for long life and stability, but it is also possible just to stack bricks on each other to create a circular type.

The construction of a permanent, brick barbeque is detailed below. Allow space for plates, as well as cooking and serving equipment. These working areas can be formed of wood or an extension of the brickwork.

With all of these designs, it is necessary to integrate a grill into the design, to provide a surface on which food is cooked. A large

---

HAITIAN INFLUENCE

Barbeque is derived from the American-Spanish barbacoa and is said to come from Haitian creole, meaning a framework of sticks set upon posts. Nowadays, the word has become synonymous with outdoor living, especially in warm climates.

---

grill, about 1m/3¹/₂ft by 50cm/20in, creates an area large enough to provide food for many people at the same time. But for average families, it need not be so large. Disused grills from abandoned domestic cookers can be used if still in good condition.

Between 13cm/5in and 20cm/8in below this is a metal grill on which wood or charcoal is burned, with a cinders tray fitted underneath. A gentle flow of air is essential under the coals, and for this reason site the barbeque so that the prevailing wind is likely to blow on the front of the grill.

Framework Concrete Pegs Hardcore

Brick base

Table

1. TO ENSURE *long life, create a firm base for the barbeque. Dig out a base about 20cm/8in deep, fill with 13cm/5in of compacted rubble then pour cement on top and level with the wooden framework.*

2. CONSTRUCT *a single, brick-thick wall, with joints staggered. Create a bay about 75cm/2¹/₂ft wide (or to suit a grill you might have). To support the grill, leave four half-bricks pointing inwards.*

3. AT ONE *end, build a wall about 60cm/2ft high, on which a wooden table can be constructed. Secure it in place by screwing four brackets (two on each side) to the wall. Use a masonry drill and fixings.*

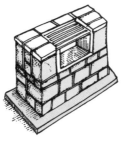

CONSTRUCT *temporary barbeques by stacking bricks one on top of another, without using mortar. But be careful when using it. Grills can be supported between bricks.*

IN CLIMATES *where barbeques are a part of everyday living, permanent types are worth constructing. Integrate areas on either side for placing trays, plates and cooking utensils.*

METAL-FRAMED *barbeques on wheels give mobility and can be stored under cover in winter. Because they do not have shelves, make a small table that can be placed next to it.*

Allow plenty of space around the barbeque and for safety reasons position it away from the dining area, especially if children are likely to be running around.

It is always useful to illuminate both the eating and barbeque areas and, if not permanently installed, this can be provided by extension outdoor cables, fittings and lights – as well as a power-breaker device fitted to cut off the current in case of accident.

4. A FIRM, *long-lasting barbeque is created, as well as a serving table. During winter, the table can be removed and stored, or covered with polythene sheeting. If the barbeque has been made from ordinary bricks, also protect these in winter by covering with polythene sheeting.*

SAFETY FIRST

Every summer, people are badly burned or killed through starting barbeque fires without proper consideration and care. All of these accidents are preventable:

- *Don't use petrol (gasoline) or any other spirits to ignite fires, and especially to revive dying fires. Although the fire may appear dead, only slight warmth will ignite petrol tipped on it, and instantaneously flames rush back and over the operator.*
- *Don't allow children or pets to go near the barbeque. Coals may look cold – but they are not.*
- *Don't just leave the fire after use – it may ignite paper, plastic cups or twigs that are blown on it. Put it out with water.*
- *Don't wear clothing that is likely to sag, billow or be blown into the fire. And for complete safety, wear protective goggles.*
- *Don't position the barbeque near houses, sheds or fuel stores. And keep a bucket of water and sand nearby in case of emergency.*

COMPOST BINS
AND DUSTBINS

❖

COMPOST bins and dustbins are frequently considered to be the unappealing parts of gardening. They are, however, vital: dustbins to remove recyclable metal and glass waste as well as other materials, and compost heaps to return decayed vegetable waste to the soil.

Most plants take food from the soil to create stems, shoots and flowers, thereby depleting the ground of plant-building chemicals. It also diminishes the soil's structure, making it less able to absorb and retain moisture. Air also becomes excluded, to the detriment of beneficial soil organisms. However, regular applications of decayed compost – either dug into the soil or applied as a mulch – replenishes this loss and keeps soil healthy.

The results of neglecting soil husbandry and continually growing the same crops on the same piece of land without adding bulky organic material can be seen throughout the world, perhaps none more notorious than the dust bowls created in North America in the 1930s, where impoverished soil was blown away during periods of drought.

In Australia, man's meddling and the removal of natural vegetation to enable mechanized agriculture to be introduced is said to be responsible for the rise in the water table. This led to saline water penetrating the topsoil and creating infertility.

Clearly, man's irresponsible care of land on a grand scale can create horrendous results. On a garden scale, neglecting to recycle plants in the form of compost is not so disastrous, but nevertheless is vital to good gardening.

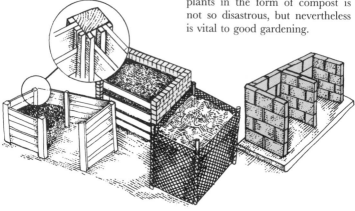

THE *materials used to construct compost bins range widely and include metal, wood, bricks, concrete blocks and wire mesh. Clearly, metal and brick constructions have a longer life than wooden types, but even these last five or more years.*

THE *optimum width and height for each bin is 1–1.2m/3^1/2–4ft, with holes in its sides to allow for the entry of air, which is essential for the decomposition of plants. Indeed, unless air circulates the compost will not decay.*

GAPS *left between wooden or metal slats enable air to penetrate, while wire-netting is even more open. Concrete bricks limit air-flow unless gaps are left between them. However, it is essential that moisture is retained in the heap, especially in summer.*

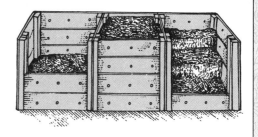

IDEALLY, three compost bins are needed: one being filled with plant material, the second completed and decaying, while material in the third one has decayed and is being used. As one is emptied, the cycle of filling and maturing changes.

CREATING COMPOST

This is formed by placing vegetable waste in layers and waiting for it to decay. At that stage, it can be used as a 7.5cm/3in-thick layer (mulch) around plants or incorporated into the soil during winter digging.

Proprietary compost bins are available, but it is quite easy to make your own: preferably, have three (see above).

Select a well-drained, sheltered position for the compost bins and spread a 25–30cm/10–12in-thick, loose layer of coarse material on the base. Straw is ideal. Tread it firmly, then form a 15–23cm/6–9in-thick layer of vegetable waste, such as annual weeds, non-greasy kitchen scraps, soft hedge-clippings, shredded cotton or woollen waste, vacuum cleaner emptyings and, in autumn, soft leaves that have fallen from shrubs and trees. Grass mowings can be used, but not in thick layers, as when wet they compact and exclude air from the heap.

Do not use thick, woody stems nor grass mowings taken from lawns that have been treated recently with weedkillers.

Next, form a 25–36mm/1–1 1/2in-thick layer of soil. Thoroughly water the heap and sprinkle sulphate of ammonia at 14g/sq m (1/2oz/sq yd). Alternatively, apply a compost activator.

Continue building up the heap in layers, occasionally sprinkling powdered chalk to counteract acidity, but not in the same layer as the fertilizer or activator. Repeatedly firm the heap to prevent it drying rapidly and water every week in summer; in winter, water only when it appears dry.

When 1.2m/4ft high, cover with 2.5–5cm/1–2in of soil, then with a plastic sheet to prevent it becoming too wet or too dry.

As the material decomposes the heap shrinks and warms up. After six to eight weeks in summer (longer in autumn and winter) use a garden fork to turn the heap. Then, leave for a further three or four months until dark and crumbly, when it is ready for use, as a mulch or for digging in.

SCREENING DUSTBINS

Screen-block walling is ideal for rapidly creating dustbin screens. The 30cm/12in-square, 10cm/4in-thick blocks are held together with a mixture of 1 part cement powder to 3 parts soft sand. The blocks need a firm base, such as a 6–7.5cm/2 1/2–3in-thick concrete slab. Allow plenty of space around the bins for them to be lifted and emptied.

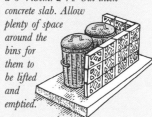

PLAY AREAS

❖

CHILDREN do not see gardens in the same manner as adults. To children they are a challenge: something to be explored and tested. To adults, as well as being areas of relaxation and beauty, they are akin to minefields, packed with potential disasters awaiting young children.

BATTLEFIELDS
OR SKILL ZONES

Children's play areas must be a balance between an army assault course and an I.Q. test. They should provide physical activities that improve stamina and co-ordination, at the same time creating mental challenges.

These are easier to provide for toddlers than children a few years older. Sandpits many evolve into rustic assault courses, with the later addition of tree-houses. And these do not have to be expensive to be enjoyable. Indeed, using a hammer and few nails is more of a challenge and satisfaction for boys than hoisting a ready-made house into position.

> ### THINK 'SAFETY'
>
> *Young children are so vulnerable that it can be a worry every time they are let out of doors.*
> - *Avoid sharp corners and edges that might trip them up.*
> - *Cover or fence off swimming pools and garden ponds.*
> - *Regularly worm dogs (see next page).*
> - *Cover sandpits when not in use to prevent cats using them as toilets.*
> - *Remove short, sharp canes from the fronts of borders.*

To children, gardens are a release from the confines of houses, somewhere where their imaginations rule and they can express themselves freely; every stick is a fantasy weapon from outer space and every brick a castle.

We do need to worry about children, but perhaps the dangers are not so intimidating as the safety tips here might suggest.

SANDPITS *have always held a fascination for children, especially when very young. Ornate and grandiose ones are easily constructed, as well as the more simple. Ensure water drains freely.*

PAVING *stones are practical edgings, as well as making ideal seats for small toddlers. However, they can create sharp edges that cause harm should they be fallen against. Buy slabs with round edges.*

RAISED *sandpits become more practical when children are able to walk. They also confine the sand more effectively and prevent it spilling or being trodden all over the garden.*

TREE *houses have a magical quality for children, perhaps offering an escape from reality. A few of these constructions look as if they have been designed by architects, while others have the nature of a washed-up raft. But whatever the design, they must be safe and strong.*

TOXICARIASIS AND DOGS

Parents shudder at the idea of Toxicara, which can damage the eyes of children. However, the chance of infection is remote. Toxicaria canis *is the common roundworm of dogs. Eggs are excreted and lie on the ground where they remain for two years. Children's fingers may become contaminated and the eggs pass into their mouths. Prevention is easy and simple:*

• *Worm your dog regularly — consult your veterinary surgeon about the dosage and frequency.*

• *Fence off sandpits and play areas used by young children. Also, cover when not in use.*

• *Remove dog faeces — scoops and plastic bags are available.*

GARDEN SWINGS

These are traditional features in a garden. Many designs are available, from a baby type where the child is constrained in a basket-like arrangement, to home-made ones where a wooden seat is suspended from two ropes.

Safety must be paramount, as accidents tend to be serious should the swing break. However, there are millions of happy swing hours each year, without any accidents or problems.

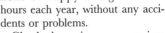

• Check the swing every spring, then every month throughout summer. Replace broken or worn parts immediately, especially ropes and chains.

• If grass has worn away from the ground under the swing, do not replace it with concrete. Thick rubber mats are available. Alternatively, lay fresh turves.

• Ensure there is plenty of space around the swing and that it does not cross a path.

FELLED *trees or large logs need not be eyesores. Indeed, they can become an attractive feature in a child's garden, creating a rural climbing frame and swing. An old car tyre tied to a stout rope makes a wonderful swing. Thoroughly wash the tyre before using it.*

USEFUL GARDEN
PROJECT TERMS
❖

AGGREGATES: *A mixture of sand and gravel. They are classified as 'coarse' or 'fine'.*

ARRIS RAIL: *Wooden rails, usually triangular in cross-section, and used to support vertical fencing boards, such as feathered types.*

BATTERED: *A wall slightly inclined to retain soil.*

BOLSTER CHISEL: *A completely metal chisel used to cut bricks and paving slabs. The width of the cutting head ranges from about 5cm/2in to 15cm/6in.*

BOND: *The arrangement of bricks in a wall or building.*

BUILDER'S SAND: *Soft sand, used with Portland cement to form mortar, and used to lay bricks and paving slabs.*

BUILDER'S SPIRIT-LEVEL: *A spirit-level, about 90cm/3ft long, made or metal or wood.*

CAPPING: *Covering the tops of walls or fences to prevent water entering and causing damage.*

CEMENT: *see Portland Cement.*

CLUB-HAMMER: *A hammer with a heavy head (about 1.5kg/3lbs). The wooden handle is usually less than 30cm/12in long.*

COMMON BRICKS: *General purpose and used where appearance is not vital. They do not have 'facing' sides and are usually painted or rendered.*

CONCRETE: *A blend of sharp sand, aggregate and Portland cement. The ratio of these vary, according to the purpose of the concrete. These are partly influenced by the possible exposure to frost.*

COPING: *The top of a wall or roof and usually slanted.*

CROSS-HALVING JOINT: *A type of woodworking joint, when part of a piece of wood is cut half-way through and a section removed.*

DAMP COURSE: *A flexible membrane – or slate – used to prevent moisture spreading up a wall from ground-level.*

DISC CUTTER: *A machine used to cut hard building materials, such as concrete slabs and bricks.*

DRESSED POLES: *Rustic poles after the bark has been removed.*

DRESSED STONE: *Slightly formal outline, but with an informal surface. However, the outline is not as clinical as when sawn.*

DRY-PACKED MIXES: *A mixture of Portland cement and aggregates in proportions to suit most jobs. Ideal for small jobs. Usually bought in bags.*

ENGINEERING BRICK: *Dense, smooth and impervious to water.*

FACING BRICK: *Use to produce an attractive finish, rough or smooth. Facing edges on sides and ends only.*

FEATHERED BOARD: *Vertical fencing boards, thinner on one edge so that they can overlap slightly.*

FLEXIBLE LINER: *Material used to line the base and sides of a pond to create a waterproof skin.*

FOOTINGS: *The supporting base or groundwork for a structure. The depth to which they are dug depends on the soil and expected weight of the wall or building.*

FORMWORK: *Another term (but more technical) for framework.*

FOUNDATIONS: *The part of a building which is below ground-level and upon which it is constructed.*

FRAMEWORK: *Use to confine concrete to a specified area and to indicate its height.*

GLASS-FIBRE: *A composite material formed of glass fibres in resin. Use to form the shells of garden ponds.*

GRAVEL BOARD: *A horizontal board used to fill an area between the ground and the base of a fence.*

HARD CORE: *Materials used to create a firm base. Must be free from wood and vegetable material. Its thickness depends on the soil and expected weight of the structure.*

HEAD OF WATER: *Used to define the distance from the surface of the lowest pond to the top of the highest one. This distance influences the power of the pump needed to operate a waterfall.*

HERRINGBONE: *A pattern used when laying bricks or pavers. There are two forms: 45 and 90 degree patterns.*

HYDRAULIC STONE-SPLITTER: *A mechanical piece of equipment (invariably hired) for cutting paving blocks.*

JOINTED TRELLIS: *Trellises where the vertical and horizontal struts are let into each other.*

MOLE DRAIN: *Created when a metal, bullet-like head is drawn through the soil, 45–75cm/$1^1/2$–$2^1/2$ft below the surface. Only suitable for large areas, such as sports field.*

MORTAR: *A mixture of soft sand and Portland cement. Used to lay bricks and paving stones.*

MOWING STRIP: *A flat surface, usually formed of bricks or paving slabs, to enable mowing machines to cut close to a wall.*

PARQUET: *A pattern used when laying bricks or pavers.*

PAVERS: *A relatively new product; weather-proof, brick-shaped and used to form drives, patios and paths.*

PIPE DRAINS: *Traditional way to create drains, formed from clay pipes laid end-to-end in trenches.*

PLASTIC DRAIN: *A new type of drain formed from plastic and laid in a narrow trench.*

PLATE VIBRATOR: *A mechanically powered machine (invariably hired) used to evenly settle pavers into a bed of sharp sand.*

PORTLAND CEMENT: *Powdered calcined rock and clay materials that form a paste with water, sand and aggregate, later setting hard.*

PROFILES: *A piece of wood, use to indicate the two edges of a trench and the position of the face side of a wall or building.*

RANDOM STONE: *Having an irregular outline and uneven surface.*

RETAINING WALLS: *A wall used to separate two levels of soil.*

RISER: *The vertical distance or each step.*

RUBBLE DRAIN: *A method of draining land, using a trench filled with rubble instead of using pipes.*

SCREEN-BLOCK WALLING: *Walling blocks, about 30cm/12in square and 10cm/4in thick, formed of concrete, with an open pattern.*

SHARP SAND: *Used in the construction of concrete and for laying pavers.*

SHOE PLATE: *A method of securing horizontal beams to a wall.*

SLEDGE-HAMMER: *A very heavy hammer-head secured to a long handle.*

SOIL-WATER: *Water that is naturally in the soil. Some soils are free-draining (sand and gravel), while others retain moisture (clay).*

SPIRIT-LEVEL: *A simple device to assess if a surface is level.*

STACK BONDED: *A bond, when one brick is stood directly on top of the one beneath. Screen-block walling is erected in this way.*

STEEL FLOAT: *A rectangular piece of metal (about 25cm/10in long by 13cm/5in wide) attached to a central handle parallel to the metal. Used for smoothing wet concrete.*

STEEL TROWEL: *An elongated, diamond-shaped piece of flat metal attached to a handle.*

SUBMERSIBLE PUMP: *A water pump designed to operate while submerged in water.*

SUMP: *An area into which water can drain.*

TAMPING BEAM: *A large, thick, plank of wood (sometimes with a handle at each end) used to level and consolidate concrete.*

TREAD: *The depth, or length, of a step.*

VINE EYES: *Pieces of metal nailed or screwed into brickwork to support wires upon which climbers can be supported. If screwed into a wall, first drill the wall and then plug with a masonry fixing or rawl plug. Earlier, vine eyes were knocked into the soft mortar then used in the construction of walls.*

WATERFALL: *One or several cascades of water flowing into a pond. Can be constructed from cement, glass-fibre units or flexible pond liner. Requires a pump to recycle water from the pond to the top of the cascade.*

WATER FLOW: *The flow of water from a pump and measured in gallons or litres per hour. The higher the pump is required to raise the water, the less its flow. Consult with specialist suppliers before buying a pump.*

WATERPROOF MEMBRANE: *A waterproof sheet placed between a battered wall (or any other type of retaining type) and rubble or soil used as a back filling. Intended to protect the wall and prolong its life.*

WOODEN FLOAT: *Similar to a steel float, but with a wooden surface.*

WATER-TABLE: *The level of water in the ground. This naturally rises and falls throughout the year according to the weather pattern.*

WATER-TUBE LEVEL: *A device for ascertaining levels over a long distance. One end of a hosepipe is secured to a peg at ground-level, then filled with water. When both ends of the pipe are full of water, they are at the same height. Inserting small pieces of coloured plastic tubing into the ends of the hosepipe makes the heights of the water easier to see.*

WEATHERED: *Term used to describe stone or wood that, after a few seasons exposed to rain, ice, wind, snow and sun, assumes a mellow appearance. Many modern paving stones are given a weathered appaerance – with irregular and rounded surfaces – during their construction. Earlier, concrete was frequently encouraged to weather rapidly by temporarily covering it in a slurry of cow manure.*

WEEPING HOLE: *An area left in a retaining wall to enable water to drain from the area behind it.*

INDEX

Aggregate 12, 17, 24, 51, 62
Alpine plants 44
Animals 6
Arbours 6
Arris rails 32, 62

Barbeques 56–7
Benches 54–5
Boarded fences 30, 32–4
Bog gardens 9
Bonds 18, 25, 62
Box 55
Bricks
  barbeques 56–7
  bonds 25
  paths 15, 22–3
  patios 14, 15, 17
  pavers 15, 18–19
  pillars 40
  pointing 25
  ponds 51
  second-hand 27
  steps 22–3
  types 24
  walls 24–5

Californian lilac 39
Carports 26, 38–9
Ceanothus thrysiflorus 39
Cement *see* Portland cement
Chain link fencing 33
Chicken wire fence 33
Children 60–1
Clematis 36, 37, 42
Climbers 39, 42
Cobbles 14, 15, 17
Common bricks 24, 62
Compost bins 58–9
Concrete 62
  drives 12–13
  finishes 13, 21
  paths 20–1
  paving blocks 15, 18–19
  ponds 50–1, 52
  screen-blocks 26–7, 39, 59
  slabs 14, 15, 20
  walls 24, 26
Conifers 39, 44, 49
Contouring 9
Coping 27, 28, 33, 62
Corrugated sheeting 38, 39
Crazy-paving 21

Damp courses 16, 24, 62
Ditches 11
Drainage
  car ports 38
  drain types 10–11
  retaining walls 29
  rock gardens 44
  sunken gardens 9
  water-table 10
Drives 12–13, 18

Dry-stone walls 28, 45
Dustbins 26, 58–9

Engineering bricks 24–5, 29, 62
English bond 25

Facing bricks 24, 62
Fences 30–1, 32–3
Firethorn 39
Fish 9, 46–7, 51
Follies 6, 7
Foundations 62
  fences 30
  pergolas 40
  walls 24, 26–9
Furniture 7, 54–5

Garden ornaments 6, 7, 17, 48
Gates 34–5
Gazebos 6, 7
Glossary 62–3
Gnomes 6, 7
Granite setts 15
Grass 9, 44
  paths 20
  ponds 46, 47
  steps 23
Gravel
  carports 38
  drains 10
  paths 20–1
  patios 17
  steps 22–3
Gravel board 31, 32–3, 62
Grottos 6, 7

Ha-ha 33
Hardcore 11, 16, 18, 24, 26, 50, 62
Hedera colchica 39
Hinges 34–5
Honeysuckle 39, 42–3
Hose-pipes 9, 46

Ivy 39

Juniperus communis 49

Kissing gates 34

Latches 34
Levelling 8–9
  paths 19, 20
  paving slabs 17
  pergolas 41
  ponds 46–50
  walls 24–5, 27
Lighting 17, 52, 57
Lilac 39
Logs 61
  furniture 54
  steps 22–3
  walls 27
Lonicera nitida 39, 42, 43

Mortar 12, 63
  paving slabs 16

ponds 47, 48, 52
walls 24–5, 26, 29
Mowers 9

Natural stone
  patios 14, 15
  rock gardens 45
  walls 25, 28–9, 33

Ornaments 6–7, 17, 48

Paths 16–18, 20–3
Patios 14–17
  barbeques 56–7
  bricks 14, 15, 17
  laying 15, 16–17
  pavers 15, 18
Pavers 15, 18–19, 63
Paving slabs 60
  benches 55
  carports 38
  laying 16–17
  paths 20
  patios 14, 15
  steps 22–3
Pergolas 40–1, 42–3
Personalizing 6, 54
Picket fences 30–1, 34
Pillars 40
Pipe drains 10, 63
Plastic drains 11, 63
Play areas 60–1
Pleasure gardens 6
Pointing 25
Ponds 9, 17, 44
  concrete 50–1
  lighting 52
  liners 46–7, 50–2, 62
  pre-cast shell 48–9
  pumps 53
  raised 17, 46, 51
Portland cement 63
  drives 12–13
  paths 21
  paving slabs 16–17
  ponds 48, 51
  walls 24
Posts 30–3, 37
Preservatives 31, 32, 42–3
Pumps 53
Pyracantha 39

Railway sleepers 22
Raised flower beds 17
Raised ponds 17, 46, 51
Ranch fences 30–1, 35
Recycling 58
Retaining walls 23, 28, 29, 54, 63
Rock gardens 23, 44–5, 49
Romans 12, 14
Roses 6, 39, 42, 43
Rubble drains 11, 29, 44, 63
Running bond 25
Rustic poles 42–3

Safety 17, 53, 57, 60–1
Sand
  sandpits 27, 60–1
  sharp 12, 16–18, 24, 51, 63
  soft 15, 16, 23–4, 48, 62
Scree beds 44
Screen-blocks 26–7, 39, 55, 59, 63
Seating 7, 54–5
Shaping ground 8–9
Sharp sand 12, 16–18, 24, 51, 63
Shingle 16, 23, 27, 44
Site preparation 8–9, 12, 18, 44
Slopes 22
Soft sand 15, 16, 23–4, 48, 62
Soil 8, 10, 12, 19, 44–5
Stepping stones 20
Steps 22–3
Stone
  animals 6
  benches 55
  patios 14, 15
  reconstituted slabs 55
  rock gardens 45
  walls 25, 28–9, 33
Strimmers 20, 23
Summer-houses 6
Sumps 11, 38, 63
Sunken gardens 9
Swings 55, 61

Tables 17, 54–5
Terraces 8–9, 14, 23
Tool hire 13, 18–19
Topsoil 8, 10, 12, 19, 44–5
Toxicariasis 61
Tree houses 61
Trellises 36–7, 43, 62

Versailles 6

Walls
  bonds 25
  brick 24–5
  capping 25, 27
  double 27
  dry-stone 28
  retaining 23, 28, 29, 54
  screen-block 26–7, 39, 55
Water-butts 38
Water-table 10, 59
Waterfalls 23, 52–3, 63
Wattle fences 6, 30
Windmills 9
Wire-mesh fencing 33
Woven fences 30
Wrought-iron
  furniture 7, 54, 55
  gates 35